Fostering Religious Literacy across Campus

Miriam Rosalyn Diamond
~Editor

D1519354

NEW FORUMS

Stillwater, Oklahoma
U.S.A.

NEW FORUMS PRESS INC.

Published in the United States of America
by New Forums Press, Inc.1018 S. Lewis St.
Stillwater, OK 74074
www.newforums.com

Library of Congress Cataloging-in-Publication Data Pending

This book may be ordered in bulk quantities at discount from New
Forums Press, Inc., P.O. Box 876, Stillwater, OK 74076 [Federal I.D. No.
73 1123239]. Printed in the United States of America.

ISBN 10: 1-58107-201-5
ISBN 13: 978-1-581072-01-3

Table of Contents

Acknowledgements

The Religion and Public Life Project is the result of collaborative efforts by the Society for Values in Higher Education and the Jesse Ball duPont Foundation. Special thanks go to SVHE Executive Director Marvin A. Kaiser and Associate Executive Director Robert A. Spivey for initiating and championing this effort throughout its implementation. Nancy L. Thomas played a major role in proposing and facilitating key portions of this program. Sally Howard Douglass, Director of Programs at the duPont Foundation, offered indispensable support, while SVHE presidents Allen Dunn and Cathy Bao Bean provided leadership in endorsing this venture.

Pamela I. Montgomery and Renee Devereux skillfully saw to it that all aspects of this enterprise ran smoothly. Richard B. Miller and A. Kevin Reinhart added their insights to those of Dunn, Spivey, Thomas and myself as Institute faculty. Special appreciation goes to the higher education representatives who participated in the retreat, engaging in exploration, sharing their vision, and supporting colleagues from peer institutions.

Personal thanks go to individuals who reviewed and provided feedback on draft portions of this work. Robert Spivey supplied proof-reading expertise, while Marla Amborn, Kuheli Dutt, Helen R. Gross, and Mary Jane Higgins served as important resources on technical details. Leslie G. Diamond, Priscilla Lasmarias Kelso, Virginia S. Lee, and Lois Calian Trautvetter graciously offered valuable perspectives and suggestions on renditions of this publication.

Many thanks to all of you.

This book is dedicated to Marvin A. Kaiser in gratitude for his many years of inspirational and sagacious leadership of the Society for Values in Higher Education.

Religious Literacy: The Project

Miriam Rosalyn Diamond
Society for Values in Higher Education

Robert A. Spivey
Florida State University

There are at least as many means of promoting religious literacy among American college students as there are types of educational institutions. In June of 2008, teams from diverse campuses across the country came together for the better part of a week to explore and develop curricular and co-curricular approaches geared for their populations, missions and environs. This initiative was sponsored by the Society for Values in Higher Education (SVHE) with funding from the Jesse Ball DuPont foundation.

Such an ambitious venture was quite in keeping with the long history of the Society. The Society originated during the 1920s in order to improve study and teaching about religion in colleges and universities, primarily by recruiting able young scholars into graduate study of religion, as preparation for faculty careers. This central mission, awarding competitive fellowships (recipients eventually known as Kent Fellows in honor of its founder, Charles Foster Kent), was throughout supplemented by other SVHE initiatives to expand and deepen religion-study in higher education. These many efforts included Faculty Consultations on Religion-Study for Colleges and Universities from 1945 to 48. Kent Fellows (George F. Thomas of Princeton, William E. Hocking of Harvard, Theodore M. Green of Princeton, Edwin E. Aubrey of University of Chicago, and Albert C. Outler of Duke) visited 53 institutions under joint sponsorship of the American Council of Education and the Edward W. Hazen Foundation. From 1951 to 1962, conferences/workshops were offered on Teaching about Religion for Undergraduates, which involved 15 experienced faculty/leaders and 50 young teachers, again sponsored by the Hazen Foundation.

In more recent years, the SVHE focus shifted from religion-study to more general values issues. The new initiatives included Summer Workshops for College Teachers (1994-present). Funded by the Luce Foundation, these sessions enabled instructors to engage issues of personal, professional and institutional values in the teaching/learning context. Another program introduced during this period was Models for Democracy: Strengthening higher education for civic responsibility and social justice. This offering was designed to develop and test model tools for higher education to use in effecting a more just democracy, and was built around core values such as integrity, diversity, social justice and civic responsibility

In 2005 the Society returned to its religion-study roots as it became more evident that religion was increasingly important in public life, both in domestic (the influence of the "religious right") and international (concerns over militant Islam) manifestations. Under the umbrella of the Democracy Project, directed by Nancy Thomas, SVHE boldly conceived and brought to fruition a "white paper" on the urgent need in this pluralistic democratic society for enhancing religion-study not so much in already burgeoning departments of religious studies but across the curriculum.

This 2006 document, the *Wingspread Declaration on Religion and Public Life: Engaging Higher Education* (see Appendix A), originated from a three-day conference at the historic Wingspread Conference Center in Racine, Wisconsin. This conference involved 20 scholars (plus numbers of others in advisory capacities) from various disciplines, backgrounds, and faith convictions, and was jointly sponsored by the Society and the

Johnson Foundation. One dominant theme of the discussion was the increasing role of religion in a variety of manifestations in the public life of cities, states, and nations – violence, corruption, demagoguery, hatred and terrorism on the one hand, and justice, compassion, citizenry and leadership on the other: Religion as a force for woe and weal demanded increasing knowledge and understanding by its citizens. From the Wingspread discussion three major concerns emerged in the form of recommendations for colleges and universities: 1) the need for religious literacy, 2) the need for religious understanding neither as advocacy nor denigration, and 3) the need to address growing student hunger for spirituality. The Declaration states that:

> The academy must examine how it teaches about religion; how it welcomes students' diverse religious views and spiritual interests; and how it factors religion into its educational programs and initiatives to strengthen deliberative democracy, all the while preserving standards of intellectual inquiry, public reason, and academic freedom... Changes in the landscape of religion in American public life provide the academy with myriad opportunities for fulfilling that role—for study, dialogue, critique, and action...We challenge colleges and universities to examine their courses and curricula to put into practice new ways to educate students about religion's dimensions and influence...

Support for our Wingspread conclusions, especially the urgent need for religion-study, came from an unexpected source, namely the 2007 publication of *Religious Literacy: What Every American Needs to Know – and Doesn't*. This best-selling argument by Stephen Prothero called for addressing widespread religious illiteracy in these United States:

> My argument concerning the academic study of religion in secondary and higher education is threefold: first, that teaching about religion is an essential task for our educational institutions; second, that the primary purpose of our teaching should be civic; and third, that this civic purpose should be to produce citizens who know enough about Christianity and the world's religions to participate meaningfully – on both the left and the right – in religiously inflected debates (p. 17).

Out of these basic conclusions the Society for Values in Higher Education created an Institute on Religion in Curriculum and Culture of Higher Education, with the backing of the Jesse Ball DuPont Fund.

Institute on Religion in Curriculum and Culture of Higher Education

The Institute was a five-day program held at a retreat center in Connecticut to engage and support the promotion of religious literacy among students both within and beyond traditional religious studies classes. Projects varied widely, from the introduction of modules, courses, and degree programs addressing the role of religion in areas such as politics, human services and environmental studies, to the creation of residential learning communities and service-learning excursions. Some participating institutions already had programs up and running; others were in the early phases of formulating and planning their proposals.

Faculty, administrators, and students from a range of institutions participated in the Institute. Large public community colleges and state universities were represented, as were nonsectarian and religiously-affiliated private colleges. Attendees came from the Northeast, Midwest, South, Rocky Mountain and West Coast regions of the United States. Some were based in major urban centers, while others were associated with smaller communities and college towns. Participants stated that they hoped to spend the time shaping and refining their projects, connecting with peers from other campuses around religious literacy, and gathering new ideas to inform their plans. Goals for the week were to engage in:

- reevaluation of the role of religion and religious literacy in higher education,
- determination and addressing of difficult questions generated by religious belief and differences in the classroom and across campus,
- creation and refinement of exemplary curricular and co-curricular model programs to enhance religious literacy,

reflecting the need of the diverse participating institutions and their students,
- development of plans to assess the learning outcomes of the proposed programs, and
- building of intercampus connections to support the process of introducing new curricula and programs.

The daily schedule began with whole group didactic/experiential sessions. These workshops addressed both theoretical and practical aspects of introducing programs on faith across campus. Topics included academic and religious freedom, religiosity versus secularism, interfaith dialogue, and assessing student learning. One of the challenges set before the group was to complement the work of religious studies departments with modules, courses and student life programs relating religion to other disciplines and experiences.

Afternoons were devoted to campus team working meetings. Participants considered target populations and articulated learning outcomes for their programs. They identified potential collaborators and resources – on campus and in the larger community – to support their efforts. They considered training necessary for team leaders and facilitators, and the publicity key to their project's success. Questions were provided to guide the discussion (see Appendix B). The results of these conversations were then shared with the larger group in the evenings for feedback, brainstorming, and discussion.

The involvement of student representatives from attending campuses was a valuable piece of the program. These graduate and undergraduate students contributed to all aspects of the gathering, attending sessions and participating in their team's planning activities. They collaborated as a group to facilitate a plenary presentation on the learner perspective on promoting religious literacy. The students were thoughtful, articulate, and bonded with each other.

Institute participants found the program beneficial. One faculty member in attendance stated:

What I valued most about the conference was the opportunity to share ideas and experiences with many thoughtful people most of whom I wouldn't have had the opportunity to meet if it hadn't been for the conference. I came away from the conference with an increased awareness of the diversity of perspectives on different issues as well as the shared concerns of people from different walks of life....The opportunity to work on our own projects, and then receive feedback from the other participants proved to be an invaluable learning experience. (Felicia Rose, LaGuardia Community College).

Following the Institute, attendees returned to their campuses to refine, advocate for and launch their respective programs. Some programs were introduced on-schedule, while others met with challenges, delays or modifications prior to realization.

This publication is a documentation of several of the campus projects nearly two years following the Institute. The narratives describe the process of introducing and conducting ventures such as co-curricular programs on religion and social justice, opportunities for students and faculty to engage in interfaith dialogue, an on-line course on applied religious literacy at the workplace, cross-disciplinary lesson plans on the role of religion in the public square, and the creation of a course on faith and environmental stewardship. It is our hope that these essays will provide inspiration and guidance for educators seeking to develop academic programs that will foster religious literacy among their students, thus promoting a more informed and better prepared workforce, society, and nation.

This modest beginning represents only a first step in what we hope will be a long, sustained development of religion-study throughout the curriculum and programs of colleges and universities – not solely by a massive production of religion scholars but by a greater awareness and competence of faculty in disciplines other than religion and student service professionals to cover religious dimensions wherever appropriate, both latent and manifest, with the same reflective, critical, scholarly skills exercised in their regular teaching, learning, and event planning.

Reference

Prothero, S. (2007) Religious Literacy: What every American needs to know – and doesn't. HarperCollins: New York.

APPENDIX A

Wingspread Declaration on Religion and Public Life: Engaging Higher Education

The Wingspread conference, Religion and Public Life: Engaging Higher Education, was sponsored by the Society for Values in Higher Education (SVHE) and the Johnson Foundation. Wingspread is an educational conference center designed by Frank Lloyd Wright and managed by the Johnson Foundation (www.johnsonfdn.org) in Racine, Wisconsin. The Society for Values in Higher Education (www.svhe.org) is a community of scholars who care about ethical issues — particularly integrity, diversity, social justice, and civic responsibility — facing higher education and the wider society. This document is reprinted with permission of the Society for Values in Higher Education.

In July 2005, scholars from public and private colleges and universities — representing diverse disciplines, geographic regions, and faith perspectives — came together at the historic Wingspread Conference Center in Racine, Wisconsin. The purpose of this gathering, entitled Religion and Public Life: Engaging Higher Education, was to discuss the growing awareness of and concern over the intersection between religion and public life and to define the role that higher education must play in response to those concerns. In an animated and sometimes difficult conversation, conference participants narrowed and defined the areas of focus. At the end of the gathering, participants agreed that the points of concern raised at the Wingspread conference call for study, dialogue, critique, and action. The academy must examine how it teaches about religion; how it welcomes students' diverse religious views and spiritual interests; and how it factors religion into its educational programs and initiatives to strengthen deliberative democracy, all the while preserving standards of intellectual inquiry, public reason, and academic freedom.

This document is a result of a collaborative effort by the conference participants while at Wingspread and through remote consultation in the months that followed. Each section begins with critical questions that scholars might ask themselves and their institutions. Following the questions are specific observations and suggestions that are intended to foster conversation rather than to serve as final or definitive answers to the questions.

Overview

Religion has always played a significant role in shaping American society. The nation's religious heritage, including its pluralism, remains deeply intertwined with American culture and identity. In recent decades, however, public prominence of religious views has grown even as the nation's religious diversity has increased. In this context, maintaining a pluralistic democracy demands a corresponding advance in our citizens' capacity to understand religious differences, as well as the ability and willingness to engage across differences of belief for the sake of the common good.

We are disturbed by surveys that reveal a citizenry inexperienced in engaging others on issues of religious and moral differences and moral debate. It is also worrisome that studies suggest that Americans are increasingly less tolerant of others' religious views while being less likely to compromise when their religious views are at stake. That all this is happening at a time when an increasingly large segment of the American public is studying in institutions of higher education raises directly the question of the academy's appropriate response to these developments.

We assume that colleges and universities serve as our nation's collective think tank and, arguably, conscience. Changes in the landscape of religion in American public life provide the academy with myriad opportunities for fulfilling that role—for study, dialogue, critique, and action. However religion is all too often confined to religious studies programs and campus ministries or accepted without critical inquiry. In this statement, we challenge colleges and universities to reexamine how religion is studied and taught. All students, regardless of their beliefs and values, need to understand how religions work. They need to know the constructive and critical appraisals of religion's historic and contemporary significance and, in particular, its impact on public life.

We call for a renewed commitment to intellectual inquiry standards, reason, and academic freedom and urge the academy to examine religion in those contexts. Further, we urge colleges and universities to be intentional about how they facilitate students' search for public purpose, self-understanding, and spirituality. We conclude with a call for further attention to the arts of a democratic citizenry. Despite different beliefs and perspectives, students — and their teachers — should be able to engage in a civic or classroom dialogue both thoughtfully and respectfully.

How might this vision be realized? There is no uniform approach, and each university will pursue its own programs and initiatives. We are particularly sensitive to the diverse missions among colleges and universities — religious institutions, non-religious private institutions, and public institutions. This statement addresses the common goal of colleges and universities: to prepare students to understand and participate in public life.

We encourage colleges and universities to consider the following framework, questions, and recommendations:

1. Religious Literacy

- What do graduates need to know about religion in a diverse democracy and global society?
- How well are we educating students for a religiously pluralistic democracy?

We recognize and value the contributions of religious studies scholars and programs at universities, but they cannot be expected to bear sole responsibility for advancing religious literacy. We challenge colleges and universities to examine their courses and curricula to put into practice new ways to educate students about religion's dimensions and influence. Students need to understand the historical relationship between religion and the disciplines — sciences, humanities, arts, and social sciences — and the professions, as well as the contemporary relevance of religion to the disciplines, the professions, and public life. Students should understand the need to adhere rigorously to disciplinary procedures for constructing hypotheses and disciplinary standards for evaluating theories and truth claims.

Higher education must direct more attention to teacher education with respect to these concerns. American elementary and secondary schools frequently avoid the study of religion partly because it is viewed as too controversial, because of the scarcity of adequately prepared teachers, texts, and tested curricula, and due to confusion or concern regarding First Amendment freedoms. Teacher training is key to addressing these shortcomings.

Religion has resurfaced in American public life and global society as a source of conflict, violence, and corruption and, conversely, as a source of personal strength, civic engagement, creative solutions, and social change. Colleges and universities need to provide students with multiple interdisciplinary opportunities to engage in dialogue and grapple with these glaring contrasts and to understand their personal and social implications.

Colleges and universities must support faculty development so that faculty will learn how to manage both discussion and critique in ways that do not advocate for or denigrate religious views. Teaching about religion requires understanding of and respect for agnostics, atheists, and secularists, as well as for a broad range of religious perspectives. It would be naïve to assume that most faculty are already fully prepared to negotiate the philosophical complexities of debates concerning the rationality of belief or skepticism, to cope with religious diversity, to teach the value of religious pluralism, or to negotiate First Amendment principles.

2. Standards of Intellectual Inquiry, Reason, and Academic Freedom

- How do academics preserve standards of intellectual inquiry, public reason, and academic freedom when faced with religiously grounded assertions?
- How can the classroom be open to religious insights without promoting or denigrating specific religious beliefs?

- What are the ground rules for civic discourse on matters of religion and public life?
- How do we encourage civility, candor, and diversity of perspectives through our educational programs?

Nearly all colleges and universities aspire to prepare students to be informed, responsible, and engaged citizens in their communities, in American society, and in a complex, global world. As valuable as religious studies scholars and programs are, they alone cannot accomplish the objectives of this Declaration. We urge the academy to consider as a framework for discussion the 1963 U.S. Supreme Court ruling, Abington Township v. Schempp, in which the court said:

> ... It might well be said that one's education is not complete without a study of comparative religion or the history of religion and its relationship to the advancement of civilization. It certainly may be said that the Bible is worthy of study for its literary and historic qualities. Nothing we have said here indicates that such study of the Bible or of religion, when presented objectively as part of a secular program of education, may not be effected consistently with the First Amendment.
> — Abington Township v. Schempp, 374 U.S. 203, 225 (1963)

The academy must preserve and enlarge its understanding of public reason by setting standards for inquiry and discourse. These standards of public reason should reflect the principles of rational discourse that lie at the basis of all academic inquiry. It is important to distinguish the ideals of rational inquiry — which are common features of many of the world's great religious traditions as well as Western philosophy and science — from both religious and secularist worldviews. Debate among worldviews is a valid, though often contentious, part of intellectual life. One of the university's most valuable contributions to democratic society lies in modeling how rational inquiry can contribute to these difficult and important kinds of public argument.

Higher education must foster a spirit of tolerance and actively champion an attitude of mutual respect and affirmation of the value of pluralism in a democracy without implicitly or explicitly privileging secularist worldviews or particular religious perspectives in the search for truth. Academics must explore ways to work with, rather than exclude, religious communities, and all parties must abide by the rules of rational, academic inquiry.

The principles of academic freedom should be applied in ways that preserve the right to subject religious assertions to critique, challenge, and appropriate standards of argumentation, proof, and evidence and that welcome religious perspectives and secularist worldviews when they are relevant to the search for truth.

Higher education must preserve the essential principles of intellectual integrity and academic freedom in the face of pressures of ideological interference, whether religious or secular, from across the political spectrum. It is particularly important to preserve the minority voice. Religious minorities have the same right to the public square as religious majorities; committed nonbelievers and passionate believers are equally entitled to academic freedom.

Colleges and universities must support public scholarship and encourage public discourse and other exchanges among faculty and students and in partnership with surrounding communities. Both scholarship and programs should address the pressing ethical and social issues in American democracy and do so in ways that result in heightened public awareness, civility, and civic engagement.

Colleges and universities must support faculty development opportunities that help faculty engage in democratic dialogue that is both probative and inclusive.

Higher education must develop and practice models of deliberative democracy that strengthen communities and society in general. The academy must also mediate conversations between those motivated by the desire for greater freedom of religious expression in the public square and those who believe that a more secular public square offers the best hope for religious freedom and inter-religious peace. Colleges and universities must be models for American democracy.

3. Students Seeking Purpose and Spiritual Meaning

- What is the responsibility of colleges and universities to respond to growing spiritual concerns among students?
- To the extent that a college or university enables students' search for purpose or spiritual quest, how does it simultaneously hold to standards of intellectual inquiry and academic excellence?
- If an institution's mission includes a commitment to educating students for personal and social responsibility, is a spiritual framework an appropriate template for student development?

In April 2005, the Higher Education Research Institute (HERI) of UCLA issued a report on the spiritual life of college students. The study revealed that three of every four college and university students say that they are "searching for meaning/purpose in life" and that they regularly discuss the meaning of life with friends. Students want to use their time in college partly to find meaning and purpose in their personal lives and their academic studies.

We recognize the tensions within academia that the study of spirituality raises. Many academics argue that secular colleges and public universities have no business facilitating students' spiritual formation; these institutions' responsibility is to provide an educational environment in which students are able to acquire knowledge, skills, and a sense of personal and social responsibility through disciplined questioning and intellectual challenges. Others respond, however, that this more limited view promotes a form of secularism that ignores the role of faculty as mentors. Students learn in the context of their personal values, beliefs, and experiences. Teaching and learning that ignores this dimension to student learning and development lacks authenticity or, worse, effectiveness. This mentor-teacher model applies to secular colleges and public universities, as well, provided the approach does not include religious formation.

We call for each college and university to examine its mission and curricula, to engage in campus-wide dialogues, and to be intentional about whether and how it helps students explore their sense of purpose and the public relevance of their academic studies.

Programs designed to address students' search for purpose and self-understanding, whether such programs be academic or non-academic, should complement and enrich a student's educational experience.

Colleges and universities must work together or with existing consortia, associations, and other structures for multi-institutional collaboration to create new courses and programs.

Researchers must study and assess how attention to spiritual development in students influences student learning.

Conclusion

The study of religion and its public relevance is a crucial dimension to liberal education. All students should engage that study in ways that affirm intellectual inquiry, reason, and academic freedom. The study of religion and public life should never compromise rational discourse on campus nor should it subvert knowledge attained through disciplinary inquiry. Challenges to disciplinary or professional knowledge and practice should be raised through reasoned debate and academically accepted methods that enrich student learning.

Colleges and universities must make a genuine commitment to deliberative democracy by making a commitment to principles of inclusiveness and respect as foundations for dissent, dialogue, and action. Without these ground rules for democratic discourse, the relationship between those motivated by religious beliefs and those motivated by other values will be defined by who is in the majority or in power, a rule that applies both in public life and on campus. This impasse is increasingly unacceptable to both the academy and the nation. It is the academy's responsibility to model a more positive, productive, and educationally sound form of engagement.

APPENDIX B

Institute on Religion in Curriculum and Culture

Guiding Questions for Campus Teams

1. *Why* do we want to address/increase religious literacy on our campus?

2. What *populations* are we targeting for programming?

3. By the end of programming on religious literacy, what do we want students/targeted populations to be able to *do*?

4. What *content* do we want to include in our programming?

5. What *process(es)* will we use?
   a. What *programming* will we provide?
   b. What will the *timing* be?

6. Who are the major *collaborators* in this project, and how will we get them on board?

7. What teaching *methods* do we want to use?

8. What *resources* will we need?
   a. What *training* will our faculty/staff need for this to happen?
   b. What *funding* will be necessary? Where can we get it?
   c. What *publicity* will ensure success?

9. How will we *measure* learning outcomes?
   a. What *procedures*/means will we use?
   b. What *tools* will we employ?
   c. What *rubrics* will we use to evaluate the results?

PART ONE – Why Religious Literacy

Religious Literacy across the Disciplines

Miriam Rosalyn Diamond
Society for Values in Higher Education

We remain a young nation, but in the words of Scripture, the time has come to set aside childish things. The time has come to reaffirm our enduring spirit; to choose our better history; to carry forward that precious gift, that noble idea, passed on from generation to generation: the God-given promise that all are equal, all are free, and all deserve a chance to pursue their full measure of happiness. - Barack Obama, Presidential Inaugural Address, January 20, 2009, Washington, D.C.

In order to grasp the full significance of President Obama's message, it is beneficial to identify the source of his reference. The meaning of this speech may be enhanced for those who note that Obama was citing I Corinthians Chapter 13, also known as the "love chapter." It is part of a statement urging a population to overcome strife and in-fighting. The reference to spiritual maturation is preceded by an affirmation of truth over inequality, and followed by a verse highlighting the core values of faith, hope, and loving charity (verses 11-13). Hope is a concept that has been closely associated with Obama; one of his books is entitled *The Audacity of Hope: Thoughts on reclaim-*

ing the American dream (2006), and it was a term often used in his campaign. Those unaware of this reference may miss the full implications and nuance of his statement.

In addition to comprehending public leaders' remarks, people who are religiously literate are better able to discern key issues in controversies over matters of public policy such as health care and marriage. Knowledge about religions provides a foundation for making sense of daily news items; for example, the national focus on revisions of Texas school system textbooks (Paulson, 2010) and controversy over the proposed burning of relgious texts (Cave, 2010). Religious awareness promotes understanding and increases comfort in interactions with individuals who follow diverse traditions. This includes the experience of working for the first time alongside a member of the Catholic church who has received ashes on Ash Wednesday, a Hindu who wears a tilak, or a Jew wearing a yarmulke. An individual listening to classical or world music can appreciate it more deeply if she is aware of the composition's spiritual inspirations. Where does this knowledge come from, this background that is key to discerning the meaning of so many aspects of public as well as personal life? And what is the role of higher education in promoting this awareness?

Why Religion

Religion permeates everything – being informed about it endows one with deeper insight regarding artistic, business, and international occurrences. People who are religiously literate are in a better position to examine and respond to individual, interpersonal, and political dynamics – from human development, the fine arts and identity studies to history, science, urban planning, public policy and health care. The ability to navigate and recognize the perspective and influence of world religions can inform collaborations, organizational management, and responses to current issues. It is a key that empowers people in addressing circumstances from increasingly diverse neighborhoods and workplaces to national and world events.

Studying religion in the context of other disciplines can also stimulate reflection and critical thinking. Stephen Prothero (2007b) cites George Marsden and Warren Nord's stance that educational institutions have a responsibility to engage learners in considering the "big questions…not only in departments of religion but also in courses in philosophy and economics and history and political science" (2007b, p. 140). In an era of significant political, business, and personal ethical uncertainty, it can be constructive for learners to explore faith-based principles intended to guide individuals and groups over time and across continents.

Opportunities exist to discuss and discern religion's influence in an array of contexts alongside the valuable scholarship taking place in departments of Religious Studies. Just as effective writing and communication are often addressed in courses that complement the lessons of English departments, religion can be tapped as a topic of study within the framework of many fields and in educational programming beyond the classroom.

In recent years, educators and policy makers have focused on articulating and assessing areas of proficiency deemed necessary for students to achieve success in the twenty-first century. Among these is the ability to discern and trace the role of religion in society as well as manifesting skills necessary to interact professionally and personally with associates who hold an array of worldviews and observe a multiplicity of customs.

One example of this benchmarking is the enGuage Report of the Metiri Group - North Central Regional Education Laboratory. The report advocates fostering student skills along eight dimensions needed to function optimally in this increasingly diverse and global society (Lemke et al, 2002 & 2003). Among the areas is "Multicultural Literacy" defined as "The ability to understand and appreciate the similarities and differences in the customs, values, and beliefs of one's own culture and the cultures of others" (Lemke, 2003, p. 13). This capacity lays the groundwork for effective communication and collaboration on individual as well as organizational levels. Similarly, the President of Canada's Society for Teaching and Learning in Higher Education has stressed the necessity for cultivating "intercultural competence" to ensure "the capacity to work effectively in diverse domestic and international settings" (Mighty, 2010, p.6). Religious literacy is a prime element of this aptitude.

Religious Literacy in Action

What does religious literacy look like? The Center for Religious Literacy website (Bogen) maintains that there are three aspects to this capability. First, there is awareness of the purpose of religion as a whole; the role it plays in personal and public life, the basic questions about human experience that it attempts to answer. Second, religiously literate individuals are versed in basic details and resources about the beliefs and customs of many world religions. Third, religious literacy encompasses the ability to critically analyze the role of faith and interactions between and among members of various groups. The capacity to determine the role of religion in belief, values, decision-making and life events can be fundamental in creating meaningful connections and interacting constructively with others in contemporary society.

The Society for Values in Higher Education's Wingspread Declaration on Religion and Public Life states that it is necessary to:

> …understand how religions work…. the constructive and critical appraisals of religion's historic and contemporary significance and, in particular, its impact on public life…. the historical relationship between religion and the disciplines — sciences, humanities, arts, and social sciences — and the professions, as well as the contemporary relevance of religion to the disciplines, the professions, and public life…(this includes) the need to adhere rigorously to disciplinary procedures for constructing hypotheses and disciplinary standards for evaluating theories and truth claims

There are several reasons an educated populace should be literate regarding world and indigenous religions. On an intellectual level, a person conversant regarding world religions is in a better position to engage in analysis of historical movements and cultural trends. For example, "…you can't effectively explore American history without teaching about the Rev. (Martin Luther) King, and (that) you can't teach about the civil rights leader without helping students understand the meaning and power of his frequent references to 'the Promised Land' and other scriptural metaphors, verses and concepts" (Mattox, 2009, para. 4). People with a grasp of America's religious foundations have a greater understanding of the values and motivations that led to many of our social movements and institutions.

This is also the case when it comes to analyzing and discussing literature. English professors at top-ranked American colleges and universities were surveyed regarding student familiarity with the Bible. An overwhelming majority (92 percent) of respondents indicated that students with a working knowledge of Biblical themes and ideas have an advantage over their peers in reading literature (Wachlin and Johnson, 2006, p. 6). The professors listed thirty-six genres for which this background is crucial to deep understanding. Among the genres listed were Medieval literature, children's books, Postmodernism and African-American poetry (p.18). In open-ended follow-up questions, a number of respondents volunteered that knowledge of other faiths is also important in analyzing literature (p. 37). Social commentators point out that Biblical narratives commonly appear in contemporary arts and media, including movies, music and comedy, and that familiarity with these themes can enhance one's experience of these arts (Mattox, 2009).

Literacy regarding religious beliefs and practices has pragmatic implications, as well. Globalization and the internationalization of workplaces have led to increased interactions among people of different nationalities and faiths. In order to communicate and collaborate effectively, it is necessary to be aware of the range of beliefs and rituals, as well as how these can affect the professional arena. A manager familiar with customs surrounding various religious holidays will be more skilled at scheduling events and meetings to maximize participation of a diverse workforce. A care provider can develop greater sensitivity and expertise in responding to patient attitudes that affect decision-making and behavior around health, illness and treatment modalities.

Competence in discerning the influence of faiths and traditions empowers interpersonal interactions outside of the workplace, as well. In neighborhoods, social, and recreational groups, religiously literate individuals may be more adept in appreciating and interacting appropriately with those whose practices differ from their own. People aware of the varieties of religious expression can be attuned to situations where religious customs may be a factor, and have a better sense of questions to ask regarding expected behavior. These include anticipating friends' dietary restrictions, supporting and comforting mourners, and associating with neighbors who observe religious guidelines regarding interactions with members of the opposite sex.

It is also important to be informed regarding the role of religion in the public sphere. One cannot comprehend the foundations of America's institutions and values without being conversant in the religious ideologies on which they are based (Wachlin & Johnson, 2005). Policy and regulations that affect everyday life are often influenced by religious convictions and practices. Legal debates impacted by religious beliefs have included stem cell research guidelines, end of life care, capital punishment, displays of the Ten Commandments on public grounds, same-sex marriage, and workers' rights to be excused from work in observance of holidays. Americans with a grasp of the religio-historical background and current perspectives surrounding such issues are better equipped to fully understand and engage in the discourse around them.

Jon Butler, professor of American Studies, states that

> ...religion is a phenomenon that must be dealt with — it's constitutive.... It's a part of American life as shown in the 'born again' Jimmy Carter, the 'faith-based initiatives' of George W. Bush, and appropriation of Islam by the terrorists who attacked America on Sept. 11, 2001... we need to think imaginatively about religion, and study how it has been used to transform the civil rights movement or Republican politics (Henderson, 2003, p.5)

There are dangers to being uninformed about religion. Religion professor Stephen Prothero warns of the consequences of an uneducated American public:

> In an era when the public square is, rightly or wrongly, awash in religious rhetoric, can one really participate fully in public

life without knowing something about Christianity and the worlds' other major religions?...This ignorance imperils our public life, putting citizens in the thrall of talking heads and effectively transferring power from the Third Estate (the people) to the Fourth (the press) (Chronicle, 2007, p. B6).

An aptitude for discerning and discussing the role of religion in contemporary life is an important component of being an involved and productive citizen.

The Situation

Unfortunately, the American populace is lacking in its level of religious literacy. Prothero comments that

Americans are not equipped for citizenship...without a basic understanding of... the world's...religions... There is doubtless a widening gap in the United States between what we actually know about religion and what we ought to know...the basic symbols, beliefs, practices, and narratives of...at a minimum, Judaism, Christianity, Islam, Buddhism, Hinduism and the religions of China (Chronicle, 2007, pp. B6-B7).

A 2009 ABC News/Washington Post Poll revealed that fifty-five percent of Americans felt they had inadequate knowledge of Islam (Polling Report, 2009). In another study conducted the same year, nearly half of those questioned were unable to identify the Muslim holy book or name for God (Pew Research Center, 2009). Two-thirds of respondents to a 2001 survey stated that they were unfamiliar with Hindu ideology and customs (Broadway, 2001, p. B09). Only ten percent of over 1,000 teenagers participating in a 2004 Gallup Poll were able to list five major world faiths. Of these students, fifteen percent were unable to name even one of these religions (Wachlin & Johnson, 2005, p. 35).

Americans' shortcomings exist regarding Judeo-Christian faiths, as well. Only seven percent of English professors surveyed nationwide in 2005 found college student familiarity with the Bible adequate to interpret literary works. Nearly half of respondents noted a decrease in Biblical knowledge over the span of their teaching careers (Wachlin & Johnson, 2006, p.

51). In a similar study, most high school English teachers questioned indicated that less than a quarter of their students had sufficient grasp of Biblical themes and ideas to comprehend literary works (Wachlin & Johnson, 2005, p. 14). A 2010 Pew Survey indicated that roughly half of Americans questioned know Martin Luther's role in religious life, the names of the four Gospels, that the Golden Rule is not in 10 commandments, and the religious affiliations of Maimonides, Joseph Smith, and the Dalai Lama. There is a significant gap between what most Americans should know and what they do know about religions.

Facing the Challenges

Because religion has such a broad-reaching effect on many disciplines and areas of life, there is value to studying it in the context of other fields. Faculty in the arts, professions, social sciences, and even natural sciences may find opportunities for students to examine the intersection between religion and their subject.

However, there are several challenges facing educational institutions and individuals who would like to do so. First, teaching about religion under the umbrella of other disciplines may be perceived as controversial. In *God on the Quad*, Naomi Schaefer Riley discloses that 8% of undergraduates surveyed nationally reported having attended classes in which references to religion were made on a regular basis (2005, p.3). She points out that "The attitude that faith and intellect are incompatible has a long history in America" (p.8). Academics - particularly those in secular and public institutions - may be concerned that teaching about faith may validate and strengthen its influence to the extent that poses a threat to scientific inquiry. There are members of the scientific community who experience religion as suppressing scientific progress while, in turn, some members of religious communities perceive scientists as challenging - perhaps even violating - core sacred beliefs. The heated debate about teaching evolution in public schools is a prime example of this conflict. After a long history of often extreme antipathy between both groups, it can be difficult for some academics to recognize the value of holding a worldview – including an avowedly atheistic one - and at the same time being versed in the ideologies and dynamics of world faiths.

Another aspect of this controversy arises from apprehension by some educators that teaching about beliefs implies indoctrinating or converting students to become religious adherents themselves. The distinction between teaching faith to promote belief and practice, and teaching *about* religion from an academic perspective, can be unclear. Faculty may struggle with means of addressing religion – particularly in the context of other studies - in an objective, impartial manner.

A second obstacle to promoting religious literacy is that educators of disciplines outside religious studies may lack background and training to address such a complex topic that does not fall within their area of scholarly expertise and inquiry. Gathering information to teach about religion as a historical force that is also dynamic and current is no trivial venture (Henderson, 2003). The prospect of locating credible resources that provide accurate information on faiths, including those with which the instructor may be minimally acquainted, can be disconcerting.

Third, religion is often a deeply personal topic, one about which students may have strong emotional reactions. Learners may express these reactions in class through resistance, withdrawal, confrontation, attempts to proselytize, or asserting details about their faith that conflict with widely held academic perspectives (Perry, 1970). It can be daunting for faculty to consider engaging students in scholarly discussion, exploration and critical thinking about a topic that holds so much personal meaning.

However, if we do not foster an understanding of religion and its influence in the world, we will be doing our citizens – and our nation - a disservice. Jon Butler says it is crucial for educators to examine:

> ... first, how religion could have survived so deeply and so aggressively in the 20th century; and secondly, how religion has survived and prospered and even changed given the nature of modernity. In what way have the conditions of modern life — anonymity, technology, the rise of the corporation, bureaucrati-

zation, the very factors that Weber thought would lead to the decline of religion — transformed the phenomena that we call religion? Have they? Shouldn't we know that? Shouldn't we know something about some kind of transformation, standing as we do amidst a world exploding with religious vitality as well as religious conflict? (Henderson, 2003, p. 6)

The objective is to identify means of doing so in a manner that is effective and in keeping with the protocols of critical thinking and intellectual inquiry.

Educational institutions are in a position to take the first step, to create programs across the curriculum and in student life that address the challenges and remedy the ignorance. They can provide direction and support for faculty who feel the risks of illiteracy outweigh concerns over broaching a complex, sensitive subject. Academies can provide opportunities for students to examine religion in the context of other disciplines and events to discern how and why it has such a broad influence. And schools can provide learners means of developing skills in communication, thoughtful decision-making, and cooperation with people from a variety of backgrounds.

In an era of increased globalization and information – as well as misinformation – the time is ripe for educators to confront concerns, address long-standing disputes, and identify means of preparing citizens to function fully in a diverse, complex world. The opportunity exists to promote awareness and tolerance over fear and ignorance, to foster communication and cooperation over suspicion and stereotyping. It is time to make the commitment to educate for religious literacy.

References

ABC News/Washington Post Poll (2009) Religion. Retrieved December 14, 2009 from the Polling Report Inc. website: http://www.pollingreport.com/religion.htm

Bogen, M. About Religious Literacy. *Center for Religious Literacy.* Retrieved December 21, 2009, from: http://home.comcast.net/~mbogen/religiouslit.html

Broadway, B. (2001) Destination: Enlightenment; Hindu Leaders Plan Visits to U.S. Cities to Discuss Principles of Faith and Deflate Myths. *Washington Post.* August 18, 2001. B09.

Cave, D. (2010) Pastor Cancels Burning of Koran. *The New York Times.* September 11, 2010. Retrieved December 2, 2010, from the New York Times website: http://www.nytimes.com/2010/09/12/us/12jones.html

Henderson, S. (2003) Teaching About Religion in Public Schools: Where do we go from here? Pew Forum on Religion & Public Life and the First Amendment Center. Retrieved December 23, 2009 from the Pew Forum website: http://pewforum.org/publications/reports/TeachingAbout Religion.pdf

Lemke, C. (2002). North Central Regional Education Laboratory's enGuage: 21st Century Skills. Retrieved December 14, 2009, from ERIC document database: http://www.eric.ed.gov/ERICDocs/data/ericdocs2sql/ content_storage_01/0000019b/80/29/cf/24.pdf

Lemke, C., Coughlin, E., Thadani, V. & Martin, C. (2003). enGauge 21st Century Skills: Literacy in the digital age. Metiri Group. Retrieved December 14, 2009, from http://www.metiri.com/21/ 21%20Century%20Skills%20Final.doc

Mattox, W.R. (2009). Teach the Bible? Of course. *USA Today.* August 17, 2009. Retrieved December 21, 1009 from USA Today website: http:// blogs.usatoday.com/oped/2009/08/column-teach-the-bible-of-course- .html

Mighty, J. (2010). Crossing Borders/Bridging Minds: Implications for Education. *POD Network News.* Spring, 2010. 7 – 9.

Obama, B.H. (2006) *The Audacity of Hope: Thoughts on Reclaiming the American Dream.* New York: Crown.

Obama, B.H. (2009) Barack Obama's Inaugural Address. *The New York Times.* January 21, 2009. Retrieved December 14, 2009, from the New York Times website: http://www.nytimes.com/2009/01/20/us/politics/20text- obama.html

Paulson, A. (2010) Texas textbook war: 'Slavery' or 'Atlantic triangular trade'? *The Christian Science Monitor.* May 19, 2010, Retrieved May 24, 2010, from The Christian Science Monitor website : http://www.csmonitor.com/ USA/Education/2010/0519/Texas-textbook-war-Slavery-or-Atlantic-tri- angular-trade

Perry, W. G., Jr. (1970) *Intellectual and Ethical Development in College Years.* New York: Holt, Rinehart and Winston.

Pew Forum on Religion and Public Life (2009) 53% Know Muslim Name for God Retrieved December 23, 2009, from Pew Research Center Databank: http://pewresearch.org/databank/dailynumber/?NumberID=861

Pew Forum on Religion and Public Life (2010). U.S. Religious Knowledge Survey. Retrieved December 2, 2010, from the The Pew Forum on Religion & Public Life website: http://www.pewforum.org/Other-Beliefs-and-Prac- tices/U-S-Religious-Knowledge-Survey.aspx

Prothero, S. (16 March 2007). Worshiping in Ignorance. *The Chronicle of Higher*

Education. Volume 53. *(28).* B6. Retrieved March 29, 2007, from The Chronicle of Higher Education Web site: http://chronicle.com/weekly/v53/i28/28b00601.htm

Prothero, S. (2007b) *Religious Literacy: What every American needs to know – and doesn't.* HarperCollins: New York.

Riley N.S. (2005) *God on the Quad: How religious colleges and the missionary generation are changing America.* New York: St. Martin's Press.

Wachlin, M. & Johnson, B. R. (2005) *Basic Religious Literacy. In Bible Literacy Report.* The Bible Literacy Project, Front Royal, VA. Retrieved December 14, 2009 from: http://www.bibleliteracy.org/Secure/Documents/BibleLiteracyReport2005.pdf

Wachlin, M. & Johnson, B. R. (2006) *Bible Literacy Report II: What university professors say incoming students need to know.* The Bible Literacy Project, Front Royal, VA. Retrieved December 21, 2009 from: http://www.bibleliteracy.org/bibcdocs/BibleLiteracyReport2006.pdf

A More Perfect Union: Religion, public life, and higher education

Nancy L. Thomas
Democracy Project, The Democracy Imperative and Everyday Democracy

The Landscape: Religion in American Life

Religion, faith, and spirituality have always been influential in American public life. Witness the Founding Fathers' opening meetings on the US Constitution with a prayer and the powerful spiritual foundation to the Civil Rights movement. It has been an uneasy alliance, however, reflected in disagreements over public funding for faith-based schools and programs, publicly displayed religious symbols, prayer in school, devotional use of the Bible in public classrooms, privacy and abortion rights, and same-sex marriage. Disputes over government regulation of matters of faith generally get resolved through the federal courts level, and the US Supreme Court generally hears one or two critical cases a year.

Although the vast majority of Americans – about 84% – believes in God or a higher power (Mitofsky International, 2002) the majority seemed to support a secularized public square as a way to preserve some level of civil discourse and social order. Over the past thirty years, however, a growing number of Americans expressed concern that the lack of religion in public life has led to social problems, among them, a troubling decline in morality, marginalization or disregard of those outside the cultural elite, and excessive individualism. Events, laws, and legal decisions on abortion, school prayer, and same-sex marriage provoked strong responses from religious camps. Angered by social and legal arrangements that, according to legal scholar Stephen Carter (1993), *trivialized* people's belief systems, those historically outside the cultural elite began to mobilize to reshape American social institutions. The role and influence of religious movements on politics and public policy has become more evident over recent years, particularly during national elections.

Partly because the Immigration Act of 1995 eliminated quotas based on national origin, the United States has evolved into one of the world's most religiously diverse nations. Non-Protestant immigrants are changing US populations. According to the most recent data reported by the Pew Forum on Religion & Public Life (2007), 23% of Americans are Catholic. Due to an influx of foreign-born adults in the US, Catholics outnumber Protestants by nearly a two-to-one margin (46% Catholic vs. 24% Protestant). The number of Buddhists and Muslims is nearly equal – 0.7%. Many of the traditional faiths – Protestants, Catholics, Jews, and Muslims – are experiencing increased numbers of constituents aligning themselves with religious orthodoxies. 26% of Americans identify themselves as Evangelical Protestants and 18% are "mainline" Protestants. This is partly reflected in the exponential growth in conservative churches in the 1990s (Goodstein, 2002). Yet while religiously-affiliated American grow more conservative, the number of Americans who claim that they are spiritual but have no religious preference has doubled, from 7% in 1991 to 16% in 2007 (Pew, 2007).

American civil society seems less than civil. In 2005, Public Agenda reported that Americans are weakening in their ethic of tolerance and are less willing to compromise with others of different beliefs or values (Public Agenda Reports, January, 2005b). Most Christian Americans describe themselves as tolerant of non-Christian religions (Pew, 2005b), but racial profiling and discrimination against Muslims, particularly since 9/11, is not uncommon (Public Agenda, 2005a). Despite their self-proclaimed tolerance, most Americans expect an escalation of the conflict between Christians and Muslims (Religion & Ethics NewsWeekly 2002). The public square appears to have become an increasingly hostile place – a contentious environment that suppresses dissent and discourages compromise, essential characteristics of a healthy and diverse democracy.

Adding to this mix is concern over religious illiteracy. A 2005 poll by the Pew Forum on Religion & Public Life demonstrates the positive correlation between education and religious tolerance: most Americans have favorable opinions of Jews (77%), Catholics (73%) and Muslim-Americans, with the notable exception being people with a high school degree or less (44%). Not surprisingly, the same poll shows that respondents with higher levels of education show substantially greater familiarity with the basic facts of Islam (Pew, 2005a). American's personal beliefs about religion have not changed much over the last twenty years, according to a Newsweek poll (Stone, 2009). Seventy-eight percent said prayer was an important part of daily life, an increase of 2 points since 1987. Eighty –five percent said religion is "very important" or "fairly important" in their lives, while another 30% describe themselves as "spiritual but not religious." At the same time, public schools barely teach religion. Students learn about the desire for religious freedom of the Pilgrims and the 1928 Scopes trial and perhaps some religious contexts for presidential elections, but schools do little to teach students about religious difference, beliefs, or facts (Pew, 2003).

Historically, Americans derived the rudiments of religious literacy and moral teaching from their own churches and synagogues. This too has changed. Today, the social influence of mainstream Protestant churches has been eclipsed by the rapid growth of new, conservative churches. The new churches and their constituents want a voice in school curriculum, as evidenced by the movement to include "intelligent design" in science classes.

Since the early 1990s, the world has witnessed a dramatic increase in religiously-motivated terrorism: on-going acts of violence between Protestant and Catholic groups in Ireland;

Aum Shinrikyo members who attacked a Tokyo subway; Osama bin Laden's bombings of the World Trade Center and the Pentagon, following years of attacks on U.S. embassies. Members of all major religions have played a role in the resurgence of religious terrorism. The combination of religion and violence is hardly new, but it is no longer geographically confined. Religiously motivated violence is more complex, diverse, and idiosyncratic than at any time in history. It calls for sophisticated study, dialogue, and global action.

These forces – the erosion of the secularized public square, religiously based demographic changes, increasing incivility and intolerance, religious illiteracy, and religiously motivated violence – might be described as "the perfect storm." Religion is a source of strength and character, and it is a source of conflict and violence. This maelstrom calls for Americans to examine the role of religion in public life, and for the academy to serve as a catalyst for this reexamination.

The Role of Higher Education

The academy is hardly immune to these dramatic changes, which challenge academics to think anew about the importance of religion in society and on campus. As sociologist Robert Wuthnow (1999, back cover) remarked, "the myth that religion has become irrelevant dies hard – especially among university faculty who consider themselves too enlightened to be bothered with religion... [but] whether we like it or not, religion must be reckoned with by any serious student of human affairs." A number of philosophical and practical questions are at issue, questions that are central to higher education's research, teaching, and civic missions.

Currently, most colleges and universities support undergraduate interdisciplinary religious studies programs (or philosophy programs that include many courses about religion). Those programs draw from history, sociology, political science, anthropology, economics, philosophy, and intercultural and global studies. Students study, for example, religious freedom and how the First Amendment protects a pluralistic society and preserves a measure of peace among religious and cultural groups and between the religious and non-religious in our society. Students might also learn about religion's civic purposes, its historic role in advancing civil rights and protecting the poor and disenfranchised. Some students might study different philosophical perspectives and comparative religions. These programs attract a small number of students. Other than religiously affiliated colleges, few schools offer programs that affect *all* students by the time they graduate. Perhaps this needs to change. If indeed more citizens view faith as a valuable antidote to a perceived decline in morality, and civic leaders no longer feel compelled to check their beliefs at the public door, then perhaps the academy needs to consider how the classroom might be open to religious insights without promoting or denigrating specific religious beliefs.

Some conservative religious groups claim that colleges and universities operate in culturally biased ways that privilege secular and liberal values and shut out or discredit all others. Several have taken legal action against what they view as widespread liberal bias. Many academics view these developments as evidence of anti-intellectualism and intolerance in public life that is threatening the very foundations of science, the search for truth, and academic freedom.

There is also the more practical question of *how* to educate for citizenship in a complex, diverse democracy. Higher education has long struggled with matters of access and equity, particularly for women and people of color. The result, some might argue, is a superficial version of citizenship. Higher education simply cannot achieve that goal by promoting, as Amy Gutmann and Dennis Thompson suggest, *toleration* in a so-called neutral procedural state. Tolerance...

> ...provides no positive basis on which citizens can expect to resolve their moral disagreements in the future. Citizens go their separate ways, keeping their moral reasons to themselves, avoiding moral engagement... Mere toleration locks into place the moral divisions in society and makes collective moral progress far more difficult...(1996.p.62).

A more assertive response is needed. Education scholars believe that learning is deeply personal, and that students study and gain knowledge through their personal lens, one that is shaped by social identity, beliefs, and life experiences. Diversity, including religious diversity, is a critical educational asset. Ignoring this dimension to student learning diminishes the quality of each student's learning experience.

Perhaps faith-based versions of a personally and socially responsible citizen provide better templates for student development. Religious conservatives argue that colleges and universities have been under the control of secular, cultural elites who promote values-neutral learning. This perspective has produced, according to legal philosopher Stephen Carter, a "culture of disbelief" (1993) that created social and legal arrangements that trivialize people's spirituality and belief systems. If the academy were to move beyond tolerating student's beliefs to actually nurturing their spiritual needs, it might improve the quality of postsecondary education overall.

In April 2005, the Higher Education Research Institute (HERI) at UCLA issued a report on the spiritual life of college students. The study revealed that college and university students have a very high level of spiritual interest and involvement. Three-fourths say that they are "searching for meaning/purpose in life" or that they have discussions about the meaning of life with friends. The same number of students expects college to help them develop emotionally and spiritually. Eight in ten students attended religious services during the past year. More than two-thirds pray and four in ten consider it very important to follow religious teachings in their everyday life. This dimension – if not expectation – of student learning, however, seems to fall into the category of "everybody's business and nobody's job." In another survey of faculty perceptions of student learning, only half of faculty members surveyed at research universities said that they structure their courses to substantially help students develop a personal code of values or ethics. And 83% responded that they focus in their courses "very little" or "some" on students' developing a "deepened sense of spirituality" (NSSE, 2008). Faculty prefer to leave the development of the "whole" student to student affairs units, campus ministry, families, and other organizations entirely. Integrating personal meaning and purpose into traditional academic units or creating new, interdisciplinary programs, remains uncharted territory for most institutions.

What should all students learn about religion and faith before they graduate? Where is the line between teaching *about* religion and teaching religion in ways that advance it? How can the academy improve the quality of each student's learning experience by recognizing that how and what students learn is shaped by their social identity, beliefs, and life experiences. How should higher education educate the next generation of engaged citizens in a religiously diverse democracy? These are some of the questions that colleges and universities need to consider and address.

The Wingspread Gathering

In July, 2005, scholars representing diverse disciplines, institutions, geographic regions, and faith perspectives came together at the historic Wingspread Conference Center in Racine, Wisconsin. The purpose of this gathering, entitled *Religion and Public Life: Engaging Higher Education,* was to discuss the changing role of religion in public life and the opportunities and challenges present in higher education. In an animated and sometimes difficult discussion, participants agreed that the academy needs to examine how it teaches about religion, how it welcomes diverse perspectives and worldviews, and how it addresses students' quest for meaning and purpose, while simultaneously preserving standards of intellectual inquiry, public reason, and academic freedom.

The conference was designed to model best practices in public dialogue and deliberation, and it was guided by the principles and practices of a national civic organization, Everyday Democracy. The group convened for dinner and spent the evening exchanging personal stories and getting to know each other. On Day Two, the group framed the issues (which had been outlined in a framing paper) and discussed how colleges and universities might respond to each. On Day Three, the group outlined the start of the Wingspread Declaration and agreed to finish it through electronic exchanges over the following six months.

The discussion that took place over the course of several days at Wingspread resulted in the group identifying three challenges to higher education: (1) promoting religious literacy,

(2) affirming standards of public reason, intellectual inquiry, and academic freedom, and (3) engaging students who seek purpose and spiritual meaning.

Religious Literacy: One of the unforeseen consequences of the separation of church and state, particularly after the Supreme Court decisions of the early 1960's, has been the continued exclusion of study about religion from public schools. School authorities have sought to avoid such controversial learning, in part as a response to pressures from the outside (both religious and secular), in part because of the scarcity of appropriate curriculum materials and of qualified teachers, and perhaps because of the continuing nostalgia for an assumed church/state consensus that was largely unexamined.

Over recent decades, there has also occurred a burgeoning of the academic study of religion at both private and public colleges and universities. Although influential in liberal arts components of higher education, religious study has remained largely inconsequential to the greater university, particularly in professional education where the majority of students are now being educated. This state of educational incompleteness results in a nation of citizens characterized by religious ignorance, an atomized spirituality, and an embarrassing naiveté. In general, our religious nation is characterized by religious illiteracy.

The Wingspread participants discussed the need for more study about religion in all its dimensions, disciplines and complexities at all levels of education. The academic study of religion most often involves studying comparative religion objectively in religious studies programs or considering religious traditions as components of cultural or area studies. These are both legitimate and useful in teaching students – generally a relatively small number – that their views might, indeed, be different from those of another. But these approaches have not proven to be adequate for teaching students to negotiate this complex, religion-infused world. To achieve this level of understanding and competency, students need to be exposed to religion across a full range of disciplines, including the sciences, humanities, arts, social sciences, and the professions. The goals for student learning might be interdisciplinary understanding, knowledge of and respect for diverse religions and spiritual views, ability to question one's own assumptions and beliefs, and an ability to engage in dialogue and to live with others across difference. This model has powerful implications for increasing critical and analytical thinking about religion among American citizens.

Academic Freedom and Public Reason: It is almost axiomatic that the academy should be the "keeper" of critical thought and reason, standards of intellectual inquiry, even on matters of culture and social order, and academic freedom. At Wingspread, the discussion included many worrisome accounts of challenges to academic freedom – such as the recent controversy at one large university that required first-year students to read portions of the Koran and religiously grounded challenges to scientific findings. It appears fairly easy to agree on academic freedom as a general principle, but application presents more difficulties.

Yet another perspective emerged at Wingspread: the academy needs to be open to a broader notion of public reason, one that protects scientific, empirical, and instrumental rationality but also considers other world views and claims based in faith traditions. At the very least, the remedy for uncritical and unreflective religious assertions in an academic setting is not the secularist exclusion of such discourse. An appropriate remedy would be the cultivation of critical and reflective religious inquiry *and* meaningful public discourse. Discourse on matters of religious importance demand not merely a spirit of tolerance but also ground rules of mutual respect and an affirmation of the value of pluralism in a democratic society.

Nonetheless, no one at Wingspread felt that faculty should in any way compromise standards of intellectual inquiry, reason, or academic freedom. Some expressed the view that students are more often coddled, that their religious beliefs and personal perspectives are not only welcome in the classroom, they all-too-often go unchallenged. A professor's job, according to one participant quoting Max Weber, is to ask "inconvenient" questions. (as cited in Gerth and Mills, 1946, p. 147). Certainly, faculty cannot disparage or humiliate a person, nor can they indoctrinate students. But they can be provocative and challenging. Indeed, it's what they should do. To the extent that this challenges a student's personal belief or perspective, so be it.

Where this conversation will go might be predictable based on statistics on more general public opinion. In 2004, only a year before the Wingspread gathering, a majority of Americans responded to a poll administered by the Pew Forum on Religion & Public Life that religious institutions should speak out on political matters. This view had been consistent for decades. The year 2008 marked a significant shift, and now a majority of Americans say that churches and other houses of worship should keep out of political matters and not express their views on day-to-day social and political matters (Pew, 2008).

Students' Spiritual Growth and Quest for Meaning: At Wingspread, questions emerged regarding whether higher education should address students' "search for meaning" as a valid, intellectual pursuit. What should the academy do if what students want to pursue does not, in the eyes of the faculty, contribute to their learning? Many Wingspread participants were highly critical of adding a spiritual dimension to traditional curriculum, expressing the view that values clarification is both anti-intellectual and beyond the scope of their jobs. Some faculty argued that the moral life is already encapsulated in a liberal education, and that those who push for a more spiritual dimension to student learning simply do not understand what faculty already do. Others worried that more traditional views of student learning fail to respect new ways of learning and the spiritual dimension as an enhancement to student learning. Matters of religion, faith, and spirituality are caught squarely in this divide.

In the end, the group wondered whether students' overwhelming focus on personal gain and career advancement nullified higher education's role as either a catalyst for public reason or spiritual growth.

In the process of examining these issues, a clear division emerged among the Wingspread participants that deserves special attention: a fundamental tension developed regarding the role of faculty and the primary function of a liberal education. When the question of attending to the spiritual dimension to student learning arose, several Wingspread participants argued that religion is best taught in ways that are values-neutral and that emphasize critical thinking and reason. Defenders of this perspective on faculty roles felt that the recent call for attending to the students' quest for meaning and related concerns for student development and civic engagement imperatives were asking teaching faculty to take on "therapeutic" functions that were inappropriate. Others disagreed, opining that attending to issues of purpose, meaning, and commitment is at the heart of the role of faculty. How this is achieved and who is responsible for it surfaced as a primary divide to be addressed as the academy moves forward on the religion and public life agenda. Perhaps the divide can be partly bridged through recognition of the primary goals of higher education, student development of knowledge, critical and analytic thinking skills, and personal and social purpose – of higher education.

A Call to a Broader Agenda

The academy needs to teach for religious literacy for the public's sake, so that when debates over educational content emerge, they are not subject to manipulation by a powerful political agenda, left or right. We might start by recognizing and acknowledging some of the critiques of secular culture. Some academics view resurgent religion as a threat to intellectual standards, academic freedom, and even to the search for truth itself. And when religion is used to inflict harm, manipulate political power, and promote propaganda based on a literalistic interpretation of the Bible, scholarly concern about commingling religion and, for example, public policy, is even more acute. But the appropriate response is not to avoid talking about religion under some misconception that that kind of research and teaching is a form of indoctrination or that it violates Constitutional limits separating church and state. *Not* addressing the influence of religion in history and society reflects a bias and is its own kind of indoctrination. Of course, the academy should always distinguish between teaching in ways that advance one religion and teaching *about* religion. Further, ignoring students' perspectives based on their faith, social identity or life experiences, is not only unrealistic. It risks bringing into the learning experience a unique and valuable perspective.

The academy needs an interdisciplinary approach to studying and discussing religion on campus and to promoting learning within and across disciplines about issues that have religious implications. We can experiment with ways to be open to the role of religion in history, politics, and society without succumbing to pressure to chill academic freedom or advance specific religious perspectives. We need to commit to deliberative democracy, which means developing models of democratic discourse that work on our campuses and in this changing society. Without some model of democratic discourse, the relationship between those motivated by religious beliefs and those motivated by other values will be defined by who is in the majority, who is in power – a rule that applies both in public life and on campus. What is becoming clear is that this impasse is unacceptable to both the nation and the academy.

References

Berger, P. L. (1999). *The Desecularization of the World: Resurgent Religion and World Politics*. Grand Rapids, MI: Eerdmans Publishing Co.,

Berlet, C. (2003). *Religion and Politics in the United States: Nuances you should know*. Retrieved January 13, 2010, from PublicEye website: http://www.publiceye.org/magazine/v17n2/evangelical-demographics.html

Carter, S.L. (1993). *The Culture of Disbelief: How American Law and Politics Trivialize Religious Devotion*. New York: Doubleday.

First Amendment Center and the Pew Forum on Religion & Public Life. (2003). *Teaching about Religion in Public Schools Where do we go from here?* Retrieved March 25, 2007 from: http://www.firstamendmentcenter.org

Friedman, T. L. (2004). Two Nations Under God, *The New York Times*, November 4, 2004, pA25.

Gerth, H. H. & Mills, C. W. (1946) *From Max Weber: Essays in Sociology*. New York: Oxford University Press.

Goodstein, L. (2002). Conservative Churches Grew Fastest in the 1990s, Report Says. *New York Times*. September 18, 2002, p. A22.

Glenmary Research Center. (2002). *Religious Congregations & Membership: 2000*. Retrieved April 1, 2007 from the Glenmary Home Missioners website: http://www.glenmary.org/grc/RCMS_2000/release.htm.

Gutmann, A. & Thompson, D. (1996) *Democracy and Disagreement*. Cambridge, MA: Harvard University Press.

Hamilton, M. (2005). *God v. the Gavel: Religion and the Rule of Law*. Cambridge University Press, May 2005

Higher Education Research Institute (2005). *Spirituality & Higher Education: A National Study of College Students' Search for Meaning and Purpose*. Retrieved August 19, 2010 from the Higher Education Research Institute website: http://www.spirituality.ucla.edu/.

Milbank, D. (2004). For the President, a Vote of Full Faith and Credit. *The Washington Post*. November 7, 2004, pA07.

Mitofsky International and Edison Media Research (2002). Special Report: Exploring Religious American. *Religion & Ethics Newsweekly*, Episode no.534 April 26, 2002. Retrieved August 10, 2010, 2010, from the Educational Broadcasting Corporation website: http://www.pbs.org/wnet/religionandethics/week534/specialreport.html.

National Survey of Student Engagement. (2008). *Faculty Survey of Student Engagement 2008 Frequency Distributions at Doctoral/Research Universities*. Retrieved August 19, 2010 from the NSSE website: http://nsse.iub.edu/pdf/2008_Institutional_Report/FSSE08%20Reports%20(DRU%20-%20CB).pdf

Pew Forum on Religion & Public Life. (2005a). *A Faith-Based Partisan Divide*. Retrieved March 28, 2007 from Pew Research Center website http://pewresearch.org/assets/files/trends2005-religion.pdf.

Pew Forum on Religion & Public Life. (2005b). *Religion & Public Life Poll, July 26, 2005. Views of Muslim-Americans Hold Steady After London Bombings*. Retrieved January 13, 2010, from Pew Research Center website: http://people-press.org/report/252/views-of-muslim-americans-hold-steady-after-london-bombings

Pew Forum on Religion & Public Life. (2007). *Religion & Public Life Poll, 2007*. Retrieved January 3, 2010 from Pew Research Center website: http://religions.pewforum.org/affiliations

Pew Forum on Religion & Public Life. (2008). *More Americans Question Religion's Role in Politics*. Retrieved January 3, 2010 from Pew Research Center website: http://www.pewforum.org/docs/?DocID=334

Public Agenda. (2005a). *Racial Profiling and the War on Terror*. Retrieved August 12, 2010 from the Public Agenda website: http://www.publicagenda.org/red-flags/racial-profiling-and-war-terror

Public Agenda. (2005b). *Religion and Public Life, 2000-2004*. Retrieved March 25, 2007 from the Public Agenda website: http://www.publicagenda.org/research/research_reports_details.cfm?list=1

Sheler, J. L. (2002) Faith in America. *U.S. News*. May 6, 2002. 42.

Stone, D. (2009). One Nation Under God? *Newsweek*. Retrieved August 12, 2010 from the Newsweek website: www.newsweek.com/2009/04/06/one-nation-under-one god.html

Wuthnow, R. (1999) As cited in Peter L. Berger, *The Desecularization of the World: Resurgent Religion and World Politics*. Grand Rapids, MI: Eerdmans Publishing Co. Back cover.

PART TWO – Campus Initiatives

Section One –
Course-specific projects

A Module on Islam

Adam Gaiser
Florida State University

The Florida State University team's project for the Society for Values in Higher Education workshop-retreat was to create a short introduction on Islam and Muslims in the form of a teaching module that could be used in a variety of different settings. For our own purposes, we needed a short module to use as the basis for teaching courses related but not exclusively devoted to Islam and Muslims (for example: history or archaeology courses on the Middle East, the first two weeks of an Islam in the modern world course, or as part of a world religions course). Ideally, it should be useful when a brief introduction to Islam and Muslims was necessary as part of a larger course, but should also be beneficial on its own (it is hoped that even secondary school teachers might find it helpful). Also important to the team was a unit on Muslims in the United States. The team – a religion professor, a historian, an archaeologist and a graduate student in American religious history - believed that, concurrent with the SVHE's goal of fostering religious literacy, the topic of Islam and Muslims remained especially relevant for American college and high school students.

Deciding what topics to address was for the most part intuitive - we all taught an introduction to Islam course in one way or another, and we all brought that knowledge to the table. There were a few discussions on what to include, but the process was fairly straightforward. The other factor was the disciplines we represented. The final product necessarily reflected the interests of the professors and graduate students who crafted them: Dr. Peter Garretson hails from FSU's Department of History, and Dr. Adam Gaiser from the Department of Religion. Dr. Cheryl Ward is now in the Center for Archaeology and Anthropology at Coastal Carolina University. Brooke Sherrard is a graduate student in American Religious History in the Department of Religion at FSU. In addition, the group enjoyed the counsel of Dr. Kevin Reinhardt of Dartmouth University's Religion Department. Dr. Reinhardt's suggestions and guidance helped to mold a more coherent and methodologically sound result.

The structure of the module itself is meant to be adaptable to different needs. We began with the creation of a four unit module that would be teachable in four one hour sessions. However, the material is also adaptable to shorter sessions should an instructor require it. Each session contains lecture notes and a power-point presentation to accompany them. The first session is devoted to basic concepts and terms, and can function as an introduction to the whole of Islam as a religion. It follows, for example, the basic terminology (introduced by Marshall Hodgson in his *Venture of Islam,* 1974) for the study of Islam and Islamicate cultures.[1] Having established the conceptual groundwork for the study of Islam, the unit then addresses basic beliefs and practices of Muslims: the notion of God, Prophets and the Day of Judgment, the Qur'an, Hadîth, the so-called "five pillars," as well as concepts like *sharî'a.* Accompanying the first session is a handout for students containing definitions of the main terms.

Session two is geared toward introducing the historical progression from the Prophet Muhammad and his early polity to the dynasties and Empires of the Islamicate world. As a simple cross-section of Islamdom through the ages, it covers the Early Prophetic and Caliphal state, and the Umayyad, Abbasid, Fatimid, Seljuk, Mongol, Mamluk, Ottoman and modern (Colonialist, Nationalist and Independent) polities. By way of showing the global inter-connectedness of the medieval Islamicate world, this section also focuses on Ibn Battuta and his travels. The accompanying power-point presentations

---

[1] See Hodgson, Marshall, The Venture of Islam (Chicago: University of Chicago Press, 1974), 1:56-67.

employ several maps in the hopes of familiarizing students with what is often the unknown geography of Islamdom.

The third session is devoted to an exploration of domestic and urban space through an architectural lens. It examines cities such as London, Baghdad and Shibam (in southern Yemen) as well as domestic structures (in Shibam and Sharja, UAE) to communicate the ways that Muslims have organized their living spaces in ways that reflect religious, cultural and physical realities. The final section focuses on Islam and Muslims in the United States, and provides an overview of the major developments and movements. This section includes discussions of the slave trade (which brought many of the first Muslims to the United States), the growth of African-American expressions of Islam (the Moorish Science Temple and the Nation of Islam), as well as the impact of post-1965 Muslim immigration to the US. This session is intended to be a counterpoint to the previous three, and makes the point that Islam and Muslims have found various ways to express their religious devotion. It is also hoped that students will find modern American expressions of Islam more familiar than their medieval counterparts.

Appended to the four sessions are extra materials that enhance the presentation. In particular, the group created a number of exercises that are intended to offer additional information, or serve as the focus of group work. The exercises include: listening to and discerning qualities of the recitation of a *sûra* ('chapter') of the Qur'an, a discussion of legal opinions (*fatwas*) using the case of smoking, an explication of the Arabic names for the stars of Orion, a calculation of one's weight using Umayyad measurements (i.e. *mithqâl* and *qirât*), a visual cut-away of what is inside the Ka'ba, a comparative scriptural exercise on religion, scripture and violence, comments on the "compatibility" of Islamic religious concerns and democratic models of governance, and an explication of the differences between Sunni and Shi'a. This material, as with the sessions, is intended to be adapted to the needs of the educator: some of it could even be used as the basis for a short class.

Finally, the group collected short videos from YouTube that deal in one way of another with Islam and Muslims. Several of the selections necessarily dealt with American or European Muslims, with a few exceptions. These include:

- Kareem Salama – A Land Called Paradise Music Video

  http://www.youtube.com/watch?v=DooppK35RrY

  This video shows a cross-section of American Muslims' replying to the question "What do you wish to say to the rest of the world?" The film highlights cultural diversity among Muslims, confronts stereotypes, points out challenges they face, and shows common experiences of being contemporary Americans.

- Global Leadership Forum 2007

  http://www.youtube.com/watch?v=mSjm2e4QAbw

  Excerpts of a panel discussion by young American Muslim leaders regarding their experiences, the role of God and Muslim traditions in their lives, and their view of interfaith relations.

- `Glenn Beck and Keith Ellison

  http://www.youtube.com/watch?v=yFkpEduQJZo

  Interview with the first Muslim elected to US Congress

Other films include responses to overt discrimination against Muslims, comments by 2008 presidential candidates about the violence in Darfur, and a pictorial representation of nations that reigned in the Middle East since 3000 BCE. All of the videos ran for ten minutes or less, making them suitable for class discussion, or simply for a short yet related diversion. Unfortunately, and due to the nature of YouTube, some of the links are now broken, or the videos have moved elsewhere. Nevertheless, the use of short video in the classroom is highly recommended, and the titles can serve as a guide for the type of material that can easily be found on the internet.

Since its introduction, the module has been well received. Teaching Assistants at Florida State University use it for World Religions classes, and have found it useful. In the first round, it was discovered that the graduate students teaching the course needed something between the existing two week and four week modules. So the modules were revised and reused in the same course the subsequent semester. It has also been successfully incorporated into a class on Islam in the Modern World.

The team's gratitude goes to the Society for Values in Higher Education for providing a forum for discussion on religious literacy, as well as an opportunity to work intensely on a project to foster such literacy. In an atmosphere of mistrust and misunderstanding of Muslims on the part of many Americans, it is hoped that the module will provide a platform upon which knowledge of Islam and Muslims may be increased. Ultimately, the hope of such a project is to create a well-informed public, and to thereby bolster the democratic traditions of the United States while insuring the fair treatment of all of its citizens.

References

Hodgson, M. (1974) *The Venture of Islam*. Chicago: University of Chicago Press. 56-67.

Environmental Stewardship – a dialog between religion and the environment

Mike Taber, Keith Kester, Peter May, and Alana Yurkanin
Colorado College

Background and Context: Colorado College's Unique Mission to the Liberal Arts

Colorado College (CC) is a Liberal Arts College founded in 1874. Located in Colorado Springs at the foot of fourteen thousand foot Pikes Peak, Colorado College provides a "unique intellectual adventure" to some 1900 undergraduate students. A highly selective four-year college, CC challenges students' academic endeavors one block at a time. Professors and students at Colorado College take advantage of this structure by often venturing outdoors, using nature as a stage for learning, or an environment for study. Colorado College has a "second campus" near Crestone, Colorado. Known as the Baca Campus, the facility offers traditional classroom space; but most importantly, the facility is a gateway to the Great Sand Dunes National Park and the diverse religious setting of Crestone, Colorado.

In 1970, Colorado College disbanded the traditional semester system of course delivery for a unique, three and one-half week "block," where students take one course at a time. Under this structure, professors are able to teach courses under a schedule that best fits the contextual learning environment that favors the discipline. Colorado College offers traditional discipline specific majors, such as chemistry, English, and Religion. The curriculum aims to provide students with necessary content knowledge to be successful in their chosen major. Colorado College does adhere to the modern liberal arts, requiring students to take one-fourth of their courses outside their major discipline.

In recent years, the block plan has fostered cross-discipline studies, such as the environmental program and feminist and gender studies. These inter-disciplinary adventures have allowed faculty to develop unique courses, with goals of challenging students in "unorthodox" liberal arts dialog. The interdisciplinary curriculum is largely based on *conceptual dialog*. For example, in the environmental program, courses are built on energy, ecology, and human adaptation to climate change. It is within this context of dialog that we developed an Environmental Stewardship course. The faculty at CC are free to develop courses at any point. The courses are usually offered for three years as "topics" courses, allowing for faculty to refine their course objectives and learning outcomes. Upon the three year period, faculty usually propose the course to the broader faculty for permanent inclusion in the catalogue.

The Society for Values in Higher Education aims to support the development of programs in higher education that foster improved dialogue about the place of religion in society, including programs dealing with the intersection of science and religion. For several years, Keith Kester has taught a Freshman Year Experience (FYE) course called, *Spirit & Nature, Religion & Science*, which incorporate two continuous community service projects. Each succeeding year's service project builds on the previous years' service project. The first and longest continuing service project is with the Colorado State Parks & Natural Areas Program in partnership with the staff at Cheyenne Mountain State Park. Students are engaged in monitoring the habitation of the Park by wildlife (specifically elk, deer, bear, and turkey)—by identifying scat and tracks—since the beginning of the development of the park six years ago—it just opened to the public a year and a half ago. The second project, begun last year, involves surveying plots of land at the Baca Campus for plant diversity and presence of native species, before and after prescribed burns, in conjunction with Peter May, the fire chief of Crestone.

As a result of this course, students gained insight and facility for analyzing both environmental and spiritual/religious issues. This was evident in their reflective journal entries, samples of which stated:

- I really loved the Carmelite monastery and all the other religious centers that we visited while at Baca. After a week of being with very spiritual people that each had a different set of beliefs I came to the realization that no one religious belief is any more valid than another. Every person is different and so is the way that they choose to worship what they believe in. There are many different paths towards salvation or enlightenment but they all lead to the same place. There were many similarities between each of the places we visited. Every religious leader that we talked to touched on the importance of environmental stewardship and taking care of the world around you. I really like the message that everyone has to live on earth and that we need to take care of our home.

- .... when talking to my parents, I realized that one of the most exciting things I can take away from this class is that spirituality, religion, feminism, and many other topics can give an entirely new underlying meaning to environmental issues. Since I want to study environmental science, and am very passionate about these issues, I am so glad I took this class to start off my studies because before I learn how to help solve these problems, the topics discussed in this class help me understand the root of the problem, and how to go about solving them from a sociological stand point.

- I feel like we truly went above and beyond in this course. Looking back at my objectives from the beginning of the year, I see many if not close to all of my goals achieved. We learned about geology, and I have definitely become a more passionate and aware consumer of this earth. We have talked about religion and learned about each other with an open attitude, but we have learned to back up our beliefs with evidence and cause us to look deeper into our spiritualities. And we have defined or come closer to understanding hard concepts to think about, words like Evil, and God.

The service projects provide a contextual opportunity for focused dialog on the conflict between the Creationists/Intelligent Design proponents and the evolutionary biologists and paleontologists. A focused, positive interaction between religious communities and environmentalists serves as a catalyst for a respectful, appreciative, common approach to protecting/conserving the natural world.

Development of a New Course

Our goal for this project was to develop an environmental stewardship course based off of Keith Kester's Freshman Year Experience course. We wanted to attract students from a diverse background in religion and environment.

All four members of the Colorado College project team participated in the SVHE Higher Education Religion, Curriculum and Culture meeting held at the Trinity Conference Center in the summer of 2008. The conference provided an opportunity for the CC team to engage in face-to-face dialog with other project teams – to learn from them – but most importantly, for the CC team to develop the project in the intended context: nature. At the conference, the CC team developed the following preamble:

Whereas our culture has been disconnected from Nature, and has, in a sense, become denatured from its roots of inspiration, and there appear to be significant changes in the balance of our climate and ecosystems, therefore

We propose that we *re-nature* ourselves through our personal religious and spiritual traditions and practices, to cultivate a creative space in which to propose solutions that encourage the successful stewardship of the Earth. As we are part of the Earth, this stewardship begins with each of us.

This *re-naturing* calls on each of us to develop a meaningful dialogue and connection with Nature.

Following the conference, the CC team developed the following learning outcomes and assessments, which were implemented in the final offering (September 2008) of Keith's freshman course:

- Students will learn how to be comfortable in the natural world and to develop a journal of personal ecological footprint
- Students will learn how to effectively connect and dialogue with Nature through utilizing each of the senses.
- Students will learn how to share their connection with Nature with other humans
- Students will participate in existing Colorado College environmental stewardship project(s)
- Students will design, and possibly implement and/or assess new Colorado College environmental stewardship projects

Assessments

- Students show proficiency in thriving in the natural world, and develop a personal journal of experience
- Students present artistic representation of their sensory experiences of Nature
- Students use appropriate means in which to share their own connection with Nature, such as publications, websites, etc
- Served community and instructor provide assessment, as well as the student
- Served community and/or instructor provide assessment, as well as the student

These outcomes and assessments became the basis for developing the topics course: *Environmental Stewardship*.

The Plan

From July 2008 to September 2008, the CC team developed a new topics course, *Environmental Stewardship*, to replace Kester's FYE course, in order to offer the course for all students, rather than just freshman. On September 25, 2008, the project team submitted the course proposal to the college faculty for approval. The course was tabled by the college curriculum committee, which asked for further refinement of the course readings assignments, and field projects. The project team decided to use Kester's FYE course, offered for the second time in fall 2008, to further develop the Environmental Stewardship concept.

September 2009 brought about the final offering of Kester's FYE course. On September 24, the CC team offered the redesigned Environmental Stewardship course for faculty approval. At this time, the faculty approved the course as a topics course, which was offered for the first time during Block C July 12 – August 3, 2010. (See Appendix for course syllabus).

Feedback from many of the thirteen participating students mirrored that of the FYE course, with comments such as:

> ...the spiritual aspect of the class — this could be the whole class in itself. For me, this is the part that I took the most from. I came away with a better understanding of my own spirituality, although maybe not as much in the way it connects to nature. Nonetheless, this was the highlight of the class, especially when combined with the BACA experience of spiritual centers.

> I think that by being able to go to and experience the different religions I was able to take what I was *reading* and learning about and place it into a real life experience.

> ...I have loved learning about religious and intellectual diversity and plurality. My mind is open and curious in new ways and sensitive to new modes of being and experiencing the world. In the grand scheme of things, I think this class will have a long-term influence on my perceptions and path.

> I understand that everyone is searching for a meaning to their life and their existence. Science and Religion offer paths to an-

swer these questions. Both seek to better understand the unknown through study and imagination. Melding the two together can offer an explanation for the unknowable as well as a
process to discover the unknowable.

Successes of the Project

The successes of the project are as follows:
- Three successful offerings of Kester's *Spirit & Nature, Reli-
gion & Science* course.
- The development of an Environmental Stewardship course
- The establishment of diverse religious collaborations at
Crestone, Colorado
- The establishment of an on-going field based research project
in collaboration with the staff at Cheyenne Mountain State
Park

The greatest success of our project to date is establishing a
service-learning project as the anchor for student learning. A
service-learning project provides contextual dialog in which
students become engaged. It is all too easy to have serious,
deeply personal and spiritual dialog in the protected confines
of a classroom. However, when two or more people work toward a common goal, they tend to step outside their comfort
zone and into one of mutualism.

Challenges and Unexpected Surprises and Benefits

Absolutely, there were challenges! Getting courses approved at Colorado College is a rigorous process. Courses must
get department approval, then division approval, then college-
wide approval by the curriculum committee *before* coming to a
vote of the faculty. The process is in place to protect the integrity of our mission and goals.

Perhaps one of the strongest benefits (although not a sur-
prise) has been the successful collaboration with Cheyenne
Mountain State Park personnel *and* the citizens of Crestone,
Colorado. Students have found that working side-by-side with
Cheyenne Mountain State Park staff on collecting ecological

data is a learning experience beyond the classroom. The staff provides practical realities that students don't often get in the confines of the classroom. Students (and the CC team) learned that we need to be patient when working on a project that is subject to natural expectations.

Future Plans

We are hoping that Environmental Stewardship evolves into a cross-discipline are of study, incorporated into the Environmental Issues Minor or into a Masters in Environmental Education with collaboration from the Religion department. These long-term goals will take time to develop. The new Environmental Stewardship course is a step in the right direction.

Appendix

Course Syllabus (Excerpts)

EV120 Topics in Environmental Science: Environmental
Stewardship; Spirituality and Nature
Keith Kester and Peter May
Block C, 2010

Course Description

Think of spirituality as that which grounds us by teaching
us what this world is, and what our role in that world is. This
course will explore spiritual understandings of the natural world
and our human relationship with it and responsibilities toward
it. The spiritual understandings explored will include the Native American, the Hindu, the Zen Buddhist, the Christian, the
Islamic, the Judaic, and ecofeminist understandings. One week
of the course will be spent at the Baca Campus where students
will visit four Crestone religious communities. How we can interact with and utilize the natural world and its resources
sustainably will be examined. Each student will determine their
own ecological footprint, and consider the sustainable human
population for this Earth. The class will engage in at least two
community service learning projects: 1) monitoring native plant
viability at the Baca campus following prescribed burns; and 2)
monitoring wildlife (deer, elk, bear, and turkey) populations in
Cheyenne Mountain State Park. Finally students will be asked
to produce a creative, artistic response to those parts of the natural world they have encountered in the course.

Course Objectives

1. Students will learn how to be comfortable in the natural world
   and to develop a journal of personal ecological footprint.
2. Students will learn how to effectively connect and dialogue
   with Nature through utilizing each of the senses.
3. Students will learn how to share their spiritual connection
   with Nature and with other humans.

4. Students will participate in existing Colorado College environmental stewardship project(s).
5. Students will design, and possibly implement and/or assess new Colorado College environmental stewardship projects.

Assessments

1. Students produce a personal, reflective journal that illustrates proficiency in understanding environmental stewardship.
2. Students present artistic representation of their sensory experiences of Nature, such as a paper suitable for publication, websites, poster, etc.
3. Students conduct data gathering, analysis, and interpretation as part of a service learning project report.

Budget

- Team taught course: One tenured CC Professor at full salary and one visiting professor, appropriate full salary based on vita.
- Field Trip and guest lecture budget of $2000.

Suggested bibliography:

Carroll, J. E. (2004) *Sustainability and Spirituality*. New York: State University of New York Press.

Darwin, C. R. (1859) Instinct. *On the Origin of Species*. London: John Murray. Chapter 8.

Goodenough, U. (2000) *The Sacred Depths of Nature*. Oxford: Oxford University Press.

Gottlieb, R. S. Ed., (2003) *This Sacred Earth: Religion, Nature, Environment*, 2nd Edition. London: Routledge, Taylor & Francis.

Hume, D. (2008) *An Enquiry Concerning Human Understanding*. New York: Oxford University Press, USA.

Moyers, B. (1991, June 17) *Spirit and Nature*. PBS Video. Available from: Mystic Fire Video, PO Box 422, New York, NY 10012.

Twain, M. (1904, 1906) *The Diaries of Adam and Eve*. Republished 1997. San Francisco: Fair Oaks Press.

Outline of Topics

Week 1 – CC Campus

Introduction To Our Science And Religious Backgrounds

What Is A Free Discussion?:

Domesticating Nature

> Introduction – Defining Nature;
>
> Defining Stewardship;
>
> Dimensions of Human Enquiry;
>
> A Balanced World? Population and sustainability
>
> Preserving biodiversity
>
> The Garden Of The Gods Field Trip.

Prepare And Share A Garden Of The Gods "Creation Story" Assignment

Week 2 – Community service learning project in Cheyenne Mountain State Park with the Colorado State Park Service

Consumerism & Religion; Sustainability & Spirituality

> Optimum Sustainable Human Population and Your Own Ecological Footprint Assignment
>
> Searching the Internet for the current status of a model of sustainability in the U.S.
>
> Assigned Journal Entry: Response to the Cheyenne Mountain State Park Project Choosing a Psalm Assignment
>
> Testing a Hypothesis re: Plant Diversity & Abundance Assignment

Religious Diversity & Biodiversity At Baca

Week 3 – Field Trip To Baca Campus

Principles Of Environmental Stewardship

Models Of Diversity & Darwin's or Your Hypothesis.

Upper and lower Willow Creek sites - plant identification; historic fire effects.

Spiritual approaches to nature: Religious Diversity and Biodiversity (Crestone Mountain Zen Center)

> Visit to the Shumeii International Institute

> Visit to the Hindu Ashram and Earth Ship;

Sacred Spaces & Times; Field Work And Data Analysis

Great Sand Dunes National Park.

Evolutionary Remembering & Religious Responses To The Epic Of Evolution.

Diversity & Abundance Of Plant Life In The Baca Campus Riparian Zone

Conducting Environmental Stewardship Assessment

Rethinking energy and environmental issues

Stewardship experience and assessment (remainder of the week): Cheyenne Mountain State Park; establishment of research plots

Week 4 – CC - Stewardship reports

Environmental Stewardship: What Is (Should Be)

Our Response To The Looming Environmental Crises?

Baca Diversity Project Poster Presentations

An Online Course in Religious Literacy

Justin Arft, Amy B. White, and
Debra L. Mason
University of Missouri

Religious Literacy: A New Need

Religion and public literacy have been intrinsically linked for nearly six centuries. Guttenberg's press and the Bible it printed seeded revolutions in education, democratic movements, and the lay religious movements that fed the Reformation (Altschull, 1984, p.6).

Religion remained the primary path toward literacy in Europe and the New World—the Bible was the text from which most people in the United States learned to read—until the late 1800s. Use of a common Bible became more complicated in the 19th century, in part because of two waves of religious revival throughout the 1800s, which included the emergence of unique U.S. sects such as the Church of Jesus Christ of Latter-day Saints and the Church of Christ, Scientist. Perhaps more important was an influx of immigrant Roman Catholics and Jews from diverse cultures, with diverse languages. With no universally accepted Bible to teach from and the creation of a public school system, McGuffey readers and similar texts replaced the Bible (Prothero, 2007).

Boston University Religious Studies Professor Stephen Prothero was not the first scholar to note the impact of the

Bible's removal as a textbook on public knowledge of religion, but one could argue he received the most public notoriety. Following the 2007 publication of his best-selling book, *Religious Literacy: What Every American Needs to Know — And Doesn't*, Prothero argued via major media outlets and academic circles that most Americans are too ignorant about religion to understand its local and global implications in civic life (Prothero, 2007).

The stripping of religion from public education—a trend that continued and accelerated especially after the 1950s—combined with declining religious practice, deeply diminished what most U.S. citizens knew about religion. The knowledge gap grew following U.S. immigration reforms in 1965, in which new immigrants brought their non-Western faiths, including Hinduism, Buddhism, and ancestral worship. Wars and political upheaval in the former Yugoslavia, Iran, the Middle East, and Africa brought immigrant waves of Muslims as well. Although religious demographics from 2008 showed three-fourths of U.S. citizens still call themselves Christians, most U.S. communities now have a visible presence of people practicing Judaism, Islam, Hinduism, Buddhism, or Sikhism (ARIS survey, 2008, and Eck, 1997).

Approaching Religious Literacy through the Professions

The increased visibility of diverse faiths in communities reaches into every aspect of professional life: in schools, in hospitals, among social worker cases, at social service agencies, in law offices, in news rooms, in boardrooms, and in the workplace. The 9/11 terrorist attacks brought a new visibility—and a challenge—to people of diverse faiths and how the country engaged them.

Courts and committees at all levels have sought to resolve religious conflict over the public funding of religious institutions, clothing, prayer, and other issues that sometimes erupt into public debate. And a handful of national organizations work to address gaps in religious knowledge of diverse religions. But for the most part, a review shows the topic of religion is largely omitted in the college curriculum and continuing development training of professionals, outside of dedicated religious studies courses or as a small component in cultural competency course work.

Religion and Professions at the University of Missouri

The University of Missouri is a public, secular, four-year university located in Columbia, Missouri. It is the flagship campus of the four-campus University of Missouri system and has an enrollment of about 30,000 students. It's among a handful of U.S. colleges with a wealth of professional schools on campus: Journalism, Law, Business, Engineering, Medicine, Veterinary Science, Health Professions, Nursing, and Education among them.

Religious literacy for professionals was addressed head-on at the University's Columbia campus since at least 2002. That year, Dr. Jill Raitt, founder of the school's Department of Religious Studies, created an honors course on "Religion and the Professions." The course used problem-based learning and case studies to address the issue of religion among the professions. The course was offered annually to freshmen honors students until 2007.

Raitt's passion for the topic led to a proposal to create a center dedicated to religion and the professions. In 2003, The Pew Charitable Trusts named the center the last of its Centers of Excellence and promised $3 million over two funding cycles. After Raitt founded the Center, Center-affiliated faculty developed discipline-specific courses in health professions and journalism, in addition to her honors course.[1] However, no course explicitly addressed religious literacy as it was defined by Prothero: "the ability to understand and use in one's day-to-day life the basic building blocks of religious traditions — their key terms, symbols, doctrines, practices, sayings, characters, metaphors, and narratives" (Prothero, 2007, pg. 11-12).

Center research supported the need for such a course on religion and the professions. In 2003, researchers for the Center on Religion & the Professions surveyed more than 400 professionals from seven professions (physicians, nurses, other health professionals, lawyers, journalists, business managers, and engineers) and 400 members of the public. More than 95 percent of professionals reported experiencing conflicts between their profession and religion. More than two-thirds said they are expected to know about and consider religious differences in their practice, while fewer than one-third believed they were adequately trained to prepare them for that responsibility.

The survey also found a disconnect with the public's views of how professionals interpret their faith and values. Nearly two-thirds of those surveyed reported conflicts with professionals involving religion, including religious discrimination at the hands of professionals. At least four out of every 10 people said professionals generally disregard the religious beliefs or practices of those they serve.[2]

Other surveys have shown that some professionals are less religious than the general population, further fueling this disconnect between the public and professional ways of viewing the word. (Weaver, et.al 2006; Schmaltzbauer, 2003). In addition, a Center review of MU's more than 3,300 courses found that fewer than 200 had some sort of explicit religious, ethical, or values component. Most courses that did have some religion content were, not surprisingly, in the humanities.[3] Few such courses existed in the sciences.

Tomorrow's Professionals Lacking in Religious Knowledge, Too

In 2008, researchers with the Center on Religion & the Professions conducted a survey of 503 students at University of Missouri to assess their level of religious literacy. Researchers adapted portions of Prothero's religious literacy quiz, which consisted of 16 questions (some multiple part) on the major tenets of world faiths and religion's interaction with U.S. culture. Questions included facts related to Christianity, Hinduism, Islam, Judaism, Buddhism, Catholicism, and the First Amendment. Students also were asked to identify their major area of study and other demographic information (Mason and Littau, 2008).

None of the groups of majors analyzed achieved a mean score at or above the 60 percent threshold set to establish basic religious literacy, meaning that more than half of the groups were, by Prothero's definition, religiously illiterate. Just over one out of every five students scored a 60 percent score (Mason and Littau, 2008).

Results from Center research and the positioning of the Center as focused on religious literacy for the professions meant the teaching of a course on religious literacy for the professions was an obvious and important initiative.

The Contextual Framework for Creating a "Religious Literacy and the Professions" course

When the Society for Values in Higher Education announced in 2007 a project to develop curricular models addressing religious illiteracy in colleges and universities, the Center on Religion & the Professions and its team from the University of Missouri was accepted to participate. Team members participated in the Institute on Religion in Curriculum and Culture of Higher Education in June 2008 to discuss its vision for the course.

A team organized by Center Director Debra L. Mason agreed that the religious illiteracy documented by Prothero was not a dearth of arcane knowledge or esoteric trivia, but a piece of an impending crisis to which professionals who serve an increasingly diverse public and in a religiously charged world are not immune. The team included one visiting scholar and one instructor in religious studies; a dual degree master's student in religion and journalism; and the center's director and associate director, both of whom were former working journalists with extensive experience writing about religion.

At the outset, the following issues needed to be resolved as the team envisioned the course and sought the course's approval at the university department and college level:
• which department would host the course
• what level: graduate or undergraduate

- how many credit hours for course
- what qualifications or disciplinary home for the instructor
- what was the marketing appeal and justification for course
- which delivery system (online vs. traditional)
- which pedagogical approach would be used
- which religions to include
- which professions to include.

Conversations to address these issues were held among team members, the chair of the Religious Studies department, and the university's department that managed online course content. Through these discussions team members learned that there was a shortage of higher-level online humanities courses. This, along with funding support from the online course department, led us to settle upon an online delivery for the course and to aim the content at the upper level (junior, senior, and graduate) to enhance enrollment. Faculty members within the Religious Studies department also sought from the beginning to assure that any new course did not replicate existing courses—such as World Religions—and that the course be strongly humanities based.

After discussions and negotiations, the team proposed a three-credit hour, 3000-level humanities (juniors and seniors) "Religious Literacy for Professionals" course that would be taught online through the Department of Religious Studies and MU Direct-Continuing and Distance Education. The course was approved in Summer 2009 by both Missouri's Religious Studies department and the College of Arts & Sciences.

The course was targeted toward both traditional and non-traditional students—non-traditional students make up a higher percentage of all online course registrations. These non-traditional students could include degree or non-degree students, the general population, and working professionals. Generally, the University of Missouri restricts traditional students from taking online courses. However, in summer, traditional students can sign up for online courses as well. This made summer an appealing time to offer the new online course, as well as the summer availability of a talented instructor who was enthusiastic about teaching the course. Schedules also dictated that the course be offered in a compressed eight-week summer session.

Because of the course's focus on the practical issues that most often lead to conflicts in professional settings, case studies showcased some religions more prominently than others. Thus, the selection of case studies affected the extent to which certain faiths were discussed. The religions most often discussed included indigenous beliefs from Southeast Asia, Islam, Sikhism, Christianity, and Judaism. Buddhism and Hinduism were discussed primarily in regard to religious holidays and dietary issues.

The Center on Religion & the Professions defines professions broadly, providing resources in 41 different disciplinary groupings.[4] However, the Center's course on religion and the professions mandated a distinct, limited number of professions. The team reviewed compelling case studies, readings, and known issues within the professions to hone in on the professions of health care, law, education, journalism, and the workplace (business). Limiting the professions assured adequate time (at least one week) for each profession, within the course's eight weeks.

Goals for Learning Outcomes

From the outset, this course was not intended as a world religions course that gave students thorough knowledge of the history, theologies, structure, or practices of world religions. Such courses are common on most college campuses. Instead, we sought to teach students how to engage and encounter religion in day-to-day life and especially in professional settings. Employing case studies was deemed a useful way to examine religious diversity in practical contexts.

One course goal was to enable students to articulate the role religion plays in their own (or intended) professions and others' professions. Another desired outcome was for students to evaluate and employ existing resources to resolve or address religious conflict or concerns—those discussed throughout the course and those they may encounter in the future. In short, we wanted students to:

- possess the knowledge necessary to behave appropriately in various religious settings;

- to react and respond with greater sensitivity to cultural and religious issues they encounter among clients, patients, customers, co-workers, and their communities;
- to engage more effectively in their personal and professional lives with those of diverse faiths.

As secondary outcomes, we expected that students would have:
· an introductory understanding of the core beliefs of major world religions and a basic familiarity with religious demographics, as pertinent to their personal and professional roles;
· the ability to recognize and assess religious myths and stereotypes as they encounter them;
· the confidence to be more conversant in religious dialogue, whether in political, personal, or professional realms.
· the capability to engage more actively in the lives of others and navigate an increasingly complex and diverse world aided by their deeper understanding of others' worldviews.

Teaching Methods and Assessment

Because the goal of the course was to provide religious knowledge to students as it relates directly to their day-to-day lives, content focused on the encounters people are likely to have in the United States and in an increasingly pluralistic society, rather than on theory and methodology of religious studies.

The primary teaching methods were required texts, readings, and "real life" case studies of how religious issues affect individuals and communities that interact with each another. Students worked in groups online to engage in problem solving and dialogue, and each student produced guided responses to each case study. Students also wrote weekly reflection papers in response to a topical prompt provided by the instructor. Case studies and readings were augmented with additional online resources and discussions.

Content included a "core knowledge" of religious traditions established by focusing on the building blocks of various traditions; basic "etiquette" needed for handling "lived" religious experience; pertinent religious, geographic, demographic, and political data; information about past and present stereotypes and misconceptions of religious traditions that may come into play in professional encounters; and resources appropriate to learning more about situations in which religious issues may arise and appropriate options for resolving those issues.

Content included examples from private and public realms within legal, medical, social work, and other professional communities. Topically, the course addressed themes ranging from food, prayer, and global politics to birth and death. Several texts were required. Excerpts, articles, and other readings were available on Blackboard, along with additional resources, group work, group discussion opportunities, and links to pertinent Web sites. Because the class was delivered online, the course employed online chats or message boards, allowing students to converse with each other and the instructor. (See sample lessons and assignments in appendices).

Required texts:

- Fadiman, Anne. *The Spirit Catches You and You Fall Down: A Hmong Child, her American Doctors, and the Collision of Two Cultures.* New York: Farrar, Strauss and Giroux, 1997
- Hicks, Douglas A. *Religion and the Workplace: Pluralism, Spirituality, Leadership.* Cambridge: Cambridge University Press, 2003 (selected chapters)
- Matlins, Stuart and Arthur Magida. *How to Be a Perfect Stranger: The Essential Religious Etiquette Handbook, 3rd ed.* Woodstock Vermont: Skylight Paths, 2003

Course assignments were weekly discussions (20% of grade), short written assignments (20%) and write-ups/analysis of case studies (60%).

We assessed learning and outcomes by administering pre- and post-tests to students in the course, as well as through traditional classroom assessment with papers, case studies, and course evaluations.

Outcomes and Assessments

An analysis of several measures showed the course achieved a significant number of the desired outcomes. We observed that throughout the course, the students acknowledged the presence of religious diversity and broadened their familiarity with an array of religious traditions and their impacts on the professions. Students reported learning how to better interact with "the other" — those whose religions and cultures differed from their own — within their own jobs, university environments, and in public/professional contexts. Based on student feedback, students left the course with a greater understanding of religions and cultures and were more astute and sensitive regarding how they might interact with people from diverse faiths in the future.

Characteristics of Enrollees

Based on feedback and class interactions, an estimated one-fourth of the 20 course enrollees worked in professions and the rest were traditional college students. Most of the professionals worked in health care; most of the students planned careers in journalism. Everyone enrolled was a University of Missouri student (as opposed to being a student earning a degree elsewhere.) Based on data from the final evaluation, 80% of those completing the evaluation were seniors and the rest juniors. None reported taking the course for their major, although one student reported taking it for a minor in religious studies. Half of respondents said they took the course as an elective and 40%said they took the class to fulfill general requirements.

Pre- and Post-Assessment

Students were administered a survey once prior to beginning the course and again after completing the course. The identical assessment tool included 25 questions about perceptions of their own religious literacy and ways religion intersected with various professions. Based on analysis of student responses on the pre- and post-tests, students generally reported an increase in their perceived religious literacy. The increase was statistically significant on a majority of the questions and approached significance on several others.

On each of the 25 measures, respondents were asked their level of agreement or disagreement, using a five-point Likert scale, with five being "strongly agree" and one being "strongly disagree." Respondents also were given the choice to choose "does not apply," although for the analysis it was coded identical with a three ("neither agree nor disagree"), since they were conceptually the same answer.

The pre-test survey was taken by 19 out of the 20 students in the course and 18 students took the post-test survey.[5] We hypothesized that enrollees would report increases in their perception of their own religious literacy after taking the course, compared to their answers at the start of the course. This hypothesis was supported. The students reported increases in the measures of perception of their own religious literacy on 18 of the 25 questions at a statistically significant level (using $p<.05$). The mean differences approached significance on four other questions.[6]

Two examples of highly significant differences were the questions "I believe religion is a cause of conflict in the way a business owner deals with employees" ($t=-5.17$, $df=17$, $M_{pre}=2.89$, $M_{post}=4.11$, $p<.01$) and "I understand the important issues in the relationship between people's faith and their profession as a teacher" ($t=-3.91$, $df=17$, $M_{pre}=3.50$, $M_{post}=4.50$, $p<.01$). (Recalling that 3 on the scale of 1-5 means the person neither agrees nor disagrees with the statement, the difference between the pre-test and post-test means clearly shows respondents going from a point in which they disagree with the statement to a point where they agree with the statement.)

Another example of a significant difference was the question "I understand the basic beliefs of most of my colleagues with whom I work ($t=-2.29$, $df=17$, $M_{pre}=3.17$, $M_{post}=3.83$, $p<.05$). The results show an increase in students' level of understanding between taking the pre- and post-tests.

Taking into consideration the small sample size and other environmental factors such as stories in the news, we feel confident arguing for causality in these findings — that participating in the course significantly increased student religious literacy — because increases were seen in perceptions of religious knowledge and context across the board. The questions on which the increase was not statistically significant may have been related to the small sample size, to students not recalling the answer they gave during the pre-test, or to random chance.

Ten of the 18 students at the completion of the course also filled out a standard course evaluation of the instruction and class. A summary of the evaluation results is below:

- 100% agreed that the course was presented clearly
- 100% agreed that the instructor was interested in student learning
- 100% agreed that the instructor taught effectively
- 100% rated the usefulness of the course as excellent or quite good
- 90% rated the amount they learned as excellent or quite good
- 70% rated the content as excellent or quite good; another 20% satisfactory
- 80% of respondents rated the clarity of course objectives as "high"

In Their Own Words: Praise for Course Content

One student reported feeling hesitant in the beginning but said in the evaluation: "I am so thankful I enrolled. I work in a very diverse setting ethnically and religiously, and this course has been the most beneficial course I have taken as an adult." The student reported working with several Muslim co-workers who take five prayer breaks a day. "Before this course, I based my opinion on ignorance. Now I admire the effort we make as an institution as well as the co-workers that are faithful to their beliefs."

A student praised the resources provided through the course, saying, "I plan to keep the required texts for my own use and already have a waiting list of people who wish to borrow *The Spirit Catches You and You Fall Down*." The student described the online lectures as "understandable and fun to read. (The instructor's) passion for the subject matter was infectious." Another reported: "Good discussions and discussion prompts."

Students also reported improving their understanding of religious beliefs and traditions in their present and future occupations. One student said, "Relating and communication with my co-workers' traditions and beliefs was (a) strategy that I learned while taking this course, and will be very beneficial at my job and at my university." Another said, "We discussed religious tolerance, law, and education, which I think will be very helpful in future occupations. It gave me a better understanding of others." The course also honed "Critical thinking skills, particularly as applied to religion and religious interactions" and students' "Understanding how it is that religion partakes in the workplace and how it should be tolerated, if at all."

One student reported that, "I will be more aware of religious interactions and my own assumptions about religion that I take with me." Another said, "I have more respect for my friends' and co-workers' beliefs and culture. I have a better understanding of different religious history, holidays, and holy days." Another reported that the class "Helps me think about whether certain religious practices should be tolerated in the workplace or not, and to what extent."

A student interviewed after completing the class said that "Learning about different cultures that I had never known existed broadened my perspective and reminded me that I must seek out other cultures in order to learn about them (not to assume that the world is what has already been presented to me)."

Course Successes: The Instructor's View

The course served as a model and offers a rudimentary assessment and guidance for later refining of the course and creating discipline-specific religious literacy courses. It served to help identify a "canon" of case studies and readings to be used in other courses. It also accomplished multiple learning outcomes: discipline specific, abstract critical thinking, and many real-world outcomes.

Medicine was a particularly successful content area. Not only are good resources available that highlight issues of religious and cultural conflict, but several students in the health-related professions are already being trained in this area. Most importantly, it is a field where people often deal with a diverse set of religious beliefs and practices.

The unit on religious accommodation sparked perhaps the most lively and, at times, heated discussion. Of all the content areas, this one most forced students to deal with their interactions with religion in the public sphere and how religion plays a role in people's lives.

Other areas such as law and education showed promise, though further development in terms of resources and case studies (preferably by specialists in those areas) are needed.

There were also some surprises and unexpected benefits of the course. The students who were also professionals were particularly engaged in the class and came away with information and insights they did not have before.

For example, after taking the class, a student who was a veteran operating room nurse realized that this topic was so important that she has started an effort to develop a cultural and religious assessment tool for nurses based on the course's content and Anne Fadiman's suggestions from *The Spirit Catches You and You Fall Down.*

Another student, a junior majoring in journalism, said she plans on holding on to the assigned texts "for life" and that her parents (both working professionals) have borrowed and read the books and said that through doing so they learned about people in their own work environments.

Performance as an Online Course

The course as an online format excelled in several areas. The accelerated and structured nature of the course kept students on top of assignments and assignments effectively guided the learning objective. Because the class moved quickly, students felt more inclined to keep up with the reading and assignments, which rendered a high quality of written work.

A major advantage of the online format was that the lack of face-to-face time forced students to do their own analysis from disparate sources. They needed to assemble the pieces themselves, which made it being a 3000-level (upper-division) course appropriate. Another advantage was that online discussion created a safer environment for discussion. People were less afraid to speak up and could refine their thoughts. The course also attracted professionals who could not attend a traditional class. Another advantage was that because the online format is so structured, it easily lends itself to developing modules and distinct units that can be built upon in the future.

The course, as an online class, was less flexible in terms of face-to-face discourse, which allowed for fewer spontaneous changes in course material or advanced guided research. It also lacked the interpersonal and non-verbal communication that adds to class discussion and richness of experiential knowledge. A disadvantage of the online format was that if some students were lost on theoretical terms, they were unable to have a face-to-face meeting to discuss the larger, abstract concepts (though such situations can often be resolved over e-mail). They were also unable to resolve questions about assignments or grading in person.

The course's workload was criticized by one student. The workload was recognized as a concern from the outset, given the need to learn about multiple religions; the need to understand professional norms and practices; and the compressed, eight-week schedule. Students disagreed on the length of reading and writing assignments in terms of their appropriateness.

Some others complained about the online component and about issues inherent in an online course, such as a heavy use of bulletin boards. One expressed confusion over how to reach the instructor via online (though the process was made clear in the course materials).

Challenges in Realization and Implementation

Finding good, topical material for the course was the greatest challenge. "Religious Literacy" as a concept is new, and often unarticulated. "Religious literacy" also runs the risk of only providing lists of facts about various religions, which are only part of understanding how religion functions for people. Religious literacy must include a more nuanced understanding of how religion is practiced and what it means to people who practice a tradition.

Because a "religious literacy" textbook does not exist, developers must be prepared to work with a broad array of resources. They also must go into the course with a solid sense of their methodological direction and not be pulled entirely into the work of any one of the disciplines required for the course.

In other words, without disciplinary focus and goals, a religious literacy course could easily become a world religions class or a cultural studies course.

Finding appropriate readings and books for such a time-limited course (eight weeks) was also a challenge.

The greatest challenge in teaching the material was finding students who were able to successfully interface with the course. Students with real professional experience or those who have experience with religious or cultural diversity were clearly the most successful in this environment. Students who were traditional college students were engaged in the basic methods, and certainly learned about religion, but perhaps were not as engaged as the students with tangible professional experience.

In addition, the interdisciplinary nature of this course required developing resources from a broad array of content areas and expertise. Therefore, the ideal developer or development team must have an interdisciplinary background or scope.

Administratively, we found it was important to start early with getting departments and institutions on board and to work out paperwork well in advance if working with multiple departments or entities. In our case, the course was proposed and developed through the Center on Religion & the Professions (affiliated with the School of Journalism), approved by the Department of Religious Studies and the College of Arts and Sciences, and offered through MU Direct-Continuing and Distance Education. It was initially proposed to be taught in spring 2009 (a full-length semester), but was postponed until summer 2009 because of the length of time it took to develop and proceed through the administrative process. Teaching the course during a compressed summer session necessitated changes in the content and assessment of the course to accommodate the shorter session.

Faculty leaders affiliated with the Society for Values in Higher Education and the Institute on Religion in Curriculum and Culture of Higher Education worked with our team during the Institute to refine the course. This included suggesting potential resources and directions, as well as approaches that considered William Perry's model for moral-cognitive development and learning, and Bloom's taxonomy, to encourage and reflect students' expanding abilities to process information.

Advice and Plans for the Future

From a development perspective, we learned that it is important to know your students, as that will determine your delivery method of the course. It is imperative to work out all of the administrative details between departments first. We also advise always aiming to balance the theoretical "textbook" readings with plenty of real-world case studies, possibly even developing your own case studies, as we did.

Developing and teaching the online religious literacy course was an opportunity to contextualize religious literacy and keep it from becoming an unarticulated or an academic "fad." To overcome these potential fates of religious literacy as a discipline, our first solution was to root it within a context that allows for exhibition of how religion is practiced by people, namely, the professions and public life.

Shifting the focus of the course away from religious facts and instead to a working knowledge of faith traditions enabled a greater likelihood of religiously literate interactions between students and people from diverse faiths. Most importantly, this context opens up the door for a variety of well-established approaches, from lived religion, to contemporary religious scholarship, to theories of secularism and pluralism, and even comparative religion methodologies. Even within these contexts, however, "Religious Literacy" as a discipline focuses on the *applied aspects* of these theoretical approaches, thus allowing for a fresh methodological approach and invention.

An aim with this course was to imbue it with "portability," meaning that its content, methodologies, and structure could be easily adaptable to other formats that can also effectively teach religious literacy. We plan to translate the course material into discipline-specific modules for insertion into existing curriculum; create profession-specific continuing education courses; and produce online resources that can be used beyond the course and the University of Missouri campus. These include developing "religious literacy toolkits." We also plan to refine and add content to the course and offer it again.

Conclusion

We conclude that there is a valid and important place for religious literacy instruction and curriculum in public higher education institutions. As Peter F. Steinfels, co-director of the Fordham Center on Religion and Culture, wrote in a letter to 2007 college graduates (Steinfels, New York Times, 2007):

It may be essential to know the basic doctrines, practices and stories of the world's great Faiths—and of atheism, too. But it is also essential to know how these believers and nonbelievers feel and think, and think about what others think about them—the kind of knowledge that requires imagination, empathy or, what college often provides, real encounters.

Courses such as "Religious Literacy for the Public and Professions" meet the need for enhanced instruction about religion's role in the professions and public life and also provide the foundation for additional opportunities to improve religious literacy.

Acknowledgements

We would like to thank several people for their contributions to developing this course and writing this chapter. Dr. Robert Baum, chairman of the University of Missouri Department of Religious Studies, offered suggestions for creating a course that met Religious Studies, College of Arts and Sciences, and humanities requirements; Dr. Jeremy Littau, former graduate research assistant with the Center on Religion & the Professions and current assistant professor of journalism at Lehigh University, provided advanced statistical analysis.

References

Altschull, H. (1984), *Agents of Power: The Role of the News Media in Human Affairs*. White Plains, N.Y.: Longman.

ARIS Survey (2008), http://www.americanreligionsurvey-aris.org/. Accessed Dec. 15, 2009.

Eck, D. (1997) *A new religious America: How a "Christian country" has become the world's most religiously diverse nation.* San Francisco: HarperSanFrancisco.

Littau, J. and Mason, D. (2008), *Time to "get" religion? An analysis of religious literacy among journalism students.* Association for Education in Journalism and Mass Communication. Chicago, Ill.

Prothero, S. (2007), Religious literacy: what every American needs to know — and doesn't. New York: Harper Collins Publishers.

Schmalzbauer, J. (2003) People of the faith: Religious conviction in American journalism and higher education. Ithaca, N.Y.: Cornell University Press.

Weaver, D, et. al (2006) The American journalist in the 21st Century: U.S. news people at the dawn of a new millennium. Oxford, U.K.: Taylor & Francis, Inc.

Appendix A

Religious Studies 3100 – Religious Literacy for the Public and Professions

Sample lessons

Excerpts from Lecture 1

Lecture One – Unit One

Welcome to Religious Literacy for the Public and Professions! As you've read in the course introduction, this course is primarily designed to introduce you to religion as it happens in the public and private spheres.

What this course is not:

1. This course is not one on world religions, though you will be introduced to many different religious traditions. In a world religions course, we would go through seven or eight of the world's major traditions and pay specific attention to their development, history, doctrines, founders, cosmological systems, etc. We would then engage in these traditions by comparing them to one another and contrasting them to one another, and, in the end, you would have a strong understanding of a handful of the world's major traditions.

2. This course is also not a basic list of facts. When some people hear the world "religious literacy," they may imagine a basic set of knowledge and terms that people need to know in order to be moderately educated on religious terminology, narratives, concepts, and practices. Again, you will certainly learn these pieces of information, and they play a large part in religious literacy, but the real action of this course involves delving into real cases about how religion influences people's lives.

What this course is:

1. An introduction to religion in the world. How is this different from religions of the world? Well, in scope, we don't set a particular priority on reaching or touching upon all the different traditions of the world. We do focus on examining

a wide scope of situations and spheres of life where religion plays a role in people's motivations, decisions, and lifestyle. In this process, you will undoubtedly learn about religion as a phenomenon and various religious traditions.

2. An introduction to methodologies: "Methodology" is just a fancy academic word for a way of doing something. This course will ultimately require you to employ a variety of methods by comparing and contrasting our cases, treating each case phenomenologically (hold tight - we'll explain this later) and critically. Perhaps the most important component of this course is the critical thinking and assessment you will employ when faced with unique, interesting, real, and challenging situations regarding religion and people.

Most importantly, this class does not assume that you know anything about religion or religions, but it does assume that you will be able to use critical thinking and analysis to deal with religious situations in the world. In a way, this class is aimed at the non-specialist for one very important reason: **we all encounter religion in our world, regardless of our particular thoughts and ideas about religion.** This fact leads us to perhaps the most important thing you can learn in the first week:

Religion is powerful. Regardless of whether or not you are a "religious" person or if you have the same beliefs as someone else, there is no doubt that religion plays an extremely important, powerful, persuasive, and formative role in many people's worlds. More than anything, this course will equip you with the tools to navigate a world where this is the case.

The rest of this lecture will prepare you with some basic knowledge and terms that will be essential for moving forward in this course.

In our first week, we have a few very important things to define and discuss so that we're all on the same page as we move forward in this class.

1. Working Definition of religion
2. Descriptive versus Evaluative methods
3. Religion in the Public and Workplace

Excerpts from Lecture 4

Lecture Four – Unit Two

Congratulations! You all just finished a very challenging and ambitious Case Study! And, you dug deep into a very challenging example of how religion, culture, public life, and the professions can interact – in this case, with some amount of difficulty.

We begin Unit Two with one goal in mind: what does it mean to live in a plural society and work in diverse professions?

At times in this unit, especially this week, we will be focusing on larger concepts within society – like "pluralism," "secular," "diversity," and specifically what that means for how religious individuals interact within a secular society. We'll also take a look at how other societies deal with these divisions.

But, most importantly, we will begin to focus on the workplace and professions themselves. I know that many of you are students and not professionals – in fact, you may not even know what profession you are going to be in. Some of you are deeply within a profession as well. Fear not! Either way, the professional world serves as the perfect microcosm for showcasing these interactions.

In the end, you will not only be familiar with a few religious traditions and how religion works – but you will be especially equipped to evaluate and deal with religious issues, conflicts, expressions, and actions as you interact with them in culture and at work.

Select chapters from Douglas Hicks' work *Religion and The Workplace* will orient you toward some of the issues that you should think about when thinking about religion in the workplace.

Below, after we've talked about some key concepts, I'll include a reading guide for the Hicks reading for the coming weeks.

"Secular"

This is one of the trickiest terms that we'll encounter in this class – largely because it means so many things to so many people. In general, the term "secular" is thought of as being something apart from or contrasting "religion." As we discussed in week one, the term religion can be very hard to pin down – so can the term secular.

One challenge to thinking of things as either secular or religious is that some traditions, as we've seen, make no division between things of the physical world and things of the "other" world. So – if everything is "spiritual" or "religious," then there's no need for the category of "secular."

Another problem with the term secular is that it has taken a particularly pejorative tone in the modern era – especially in certain Christian and Muslim communities. In this context, sometimes religious people think of secular as "worldly." If your religious tradition has a negative attitude toward things that are "worldly," then all things secular, from this viewpoint might be bad.

Another way to think about secular, which I will encourage in this class, comes out of a perspective on governance. What this means is that "secular" institutions are those that are not "religious" from the standpoint of the U.S. Constitution's establishment clause. We will talk about this much more during weeks seven and eight, but there is an important fact that comes out of all this:

The United States does two things:

1) Disallows the government to "establish" any laws that endorse or support or become "entangled" in any particular religious tradition.

2) Guarantees freedom of religion (1st Amendment and Free Exercise Clause)

Interesting paradox? This arrangement is interesting because it prevents the government from getting too involved with religion, but it also allows and, some might argue, encourages people to be religious.

This segues us to our next topic, perhaps one of the most important in the class:

"Pluralism"

Pluralism, simply, means an arrangement of many, or plural, types of people, viewpoints, etc. in any one system. Pluralism, in many ways, characterizes the American experience and, most importantly, characterizes the workplace.

One of the best reasons to consider the workplace and professions in order to understand religion is that the workplace "forces" or "invites" pluralism. When a company hires someone, it may not ask any questions about religious belief – or, when someone goes to a hospital or a government office, there may be no screening process that asks about a person's religious beliefs. So – not only does pluralism happen in the "public sphere," but it also happens in the workplace. It is quite conceivable to walk into a business office or a university and find representatives of every major world religion working side by side.

The workplace, then, becomes an even smaller "melting pot" where interactions and "engagements" are far more likely.

To continue this discussion, I am going to direct you, via this week's discussion, to some of Diana Eck's thoughts on pluralism. Diana Eck runs Harvard's Pluralism Project and has developed numerous resources on the subject.

"Civil Discourse"

"Civil Discourse" or "Public Discourse" are terms with which we should become familiar. In general, this refers to the types of conversations that occur within a plural environment. These conversations are inevitable. (Also, the word "conversations" here is also a bit of a coded word. You could even interpret it as "interactions" or "engagements").

The bottom line is this – if you are Christian and you work with a Muslim (insert any other combination of worldviews here), you may have conversations about the weather, the news, etc., and religion may never come up. However, religion is such a powerful dimension of people's lives that in order to have real engagement and real interaction, you may have conversations about ethics, values, even religion explicitly – or, you may be invited to a family celebration or event. In all cases, you will be interacting with or having a conversation with a set of values that may be different from yours.

Appendix B

Religious Studies 3100 – Religious Literacy for the Public and Professions

Sample Case Study: instructions and writing prompts

This Case Study is intended to be a culmination of the course up to this point. It has four goals and should be 5-6 pages when completed:

1) To engage you with the importance of religion, religious literacy, and cultural conflict/engagement
2) To engage you with a real-world example of a conflict that occurs within a professional setting
3) To get you thinking critically about how to solve problems and engage these types of situations.
4) To get you looking for additional occurrences of interactions in the professions

Below, you will find part-by-part guidelines for the write-up. Please don't be intimidated by all the parts and questions below – they truly are intended as *guidelines* to accomplish the goals above.

However, get started early! Work on this piece by piece. Though the discussion in the course is very important for this, you can start working on this as soon as you get it. If you leave this for the night before, you might find yourself in a bad place! Make it easy on yourself, and please let me know if you have any questions or concerns.

Part One: Discussion Assessment

During the last two weeks, you've all discussed issues involving cultural identity, religious belief, and the way these beliefs and values come into play in the medical professions. In a <u>concise</u> statement at the beginning of your write-up, address the following:

1. What was your group's general assessment of these challenges? Was there a variety of conversation or did you all resound on a single conclusion? (Write about this in a way

that shows you are reflecting on the discourse that you have created. Much of the learning in this class is based on the knowledge that you create through discussion.)

Part Two: Your Assessment of the Conflict

This portion of the Case Study write-up is for your own analysis and you will need to have read the material, reflected on the discussions, and be familiar with the concepts in the lectures up to this point.

1. (Briefly address) After reading the chapters on cultural and religious identity (2, 4, 6, 8, 10, 12), what do you feel are the most central and challenging issues for people of one set of beliefs encountering a different world?
2. After reading the more medical-specific chapters (3, 5, 7, 9, 11, 15) and dealing with them in discussion address the following (again, you don't have to answer each question independently, but you should use all the questions as a guide to address the central issue) (Chapter 15 may be especially helpful here):

What are the Western Medical system and the Hmong's attitudes towards healing and quality of life? How are they determined? What are their bottom lines? How can these two worlds work together? How much is it the medical and social services community's responsibility to determine quality of life, and what if their ideas of quality of life conflict with another worldview?

In short, what is that nature of the conflict between the Hmong and the Medical System?

Part Three: Solution and Engagement

Read Chapters 17 and 18. The following are simple questions, but require thought and engagement on your part. This case is a very complex and challenging case, so I will expect that you grapple with these questions as such.

1. What solution or type of engagement is Fadiman proposing?
2. What solution or type of engagement with this kind of situation would you propose?

3. How is this solution or engagement useful in your profession/future profession/or in public life? Is it practical?

Part Four: Ethics

After you have consulted the AMA's guidelines and read the Hippocratic Oath, do you think that either of these guidelines a) encourages the solution you/Fadiman proposes or b) hinders it? Does the existing language support the type of cultural sensitivity needed? Does it allow for alternative or creative approaches to the problem?

Part Five: Getting out of the case and into the world:

Read through the outline of general issues involving religion and medicine and choose one example that you find interesting (or you may find one yourself).

Once you've done this, do a Web search looking for recent news articles or commentaries that deal with one of these issues involving medicine and religion.

Once you've found an article, go to the "Discussion Board" and go to the forum titled "Medical Cases." Create your own thread and title it based on your article. Then, copy and paste a link to the article in your thread and briefly address both of the following in the thread:
1. How is this case similar or different to the case that you've just dealt with (Fadiman's book)?
2. Having learned everything up to this point, what is you brief assessment of how this case should be handled or approached?

Appendix C

Pre- and Post-test Results

The mean values of 18 students' responses to an identical pre- and post-test were calculated. A paired samples t-test was run to determine significance of the differences on each question between the pre- and post-test. Paired t-test with n=18; df=17; p<.05.

Question Number	Question Content	Significant? ✓ = yes	Mean Response (1-5)	Paired sample mean difference Pre-Post	Paired Sample s.d.	t value	Significance (p=<.05)
1	PR1 I understand the basic beliefs of my own religion or tradition, (if I have one). [pre-test]		4.39				
	PO1 I understand the basic beliefs of my own religion or tradition, (if I have one). [post-test]		4.44	-.056	1.056	-.223	.826
2	PR2 I understand the basic beliefs of most of my colleagues with whom I work.	✓	3.17				
	PO2 I understand the basic beliefs of most of my colleagues with whom I work.		3.83	-.667	1.027	-2.287	.035
3	PR3 I understand the basic beliefs of the people with whom I interact on a daily basis		3.67				
	PO3 I understand the basic beliefs of the people with whom I interact on a daily basis		3.83	-.167	1.043	-.678	.507
4	PR4 I understand the major/important issues in the relationship between people's faith and their medical treatment.		4.00				
	PO4 I understand the major/important issues in the relationship between people's faith and their medical treatment.		4.50	-.500	1.043	-2.034	.058
5	PR5 I understand the important issues in the relationship between people's faith and how it is portrayed in the media.	✓	3.78				
	PO5 I understand the important issues in the relationship between people's faith and how it is portrayed in the media.		4.56	-.778	1.114	-2.961	.009

Question Content	Significant? ✓ = yes	Mean Response (1-5)	Paired sample mean difference Pre-Post	Paired Sample s.d.	t value	Significance (p=<.05)
PR6 I understand the important issues in the relationship between people's faith and their dealings with lawyers.	✓	2.94	-1.0	1.645	-2.579	.020
PO6 I understand the important issues in the relationship between people's faith and their dealings with lawyers.		3.94				
PR7 I understand the important issues in the relationship between people's faith and their dealings with banks.	✓	2.67	-.667	1.328	-2.129	.048
PO7 I understand the important issues in the relationship between people's faith and their dealings with banks.		3.33				
PR8 I understand the important issues in the relationship between people's faith and their dealings with service employees and workers (i.e. taxi drivers).	✓	3.28	-1.389	1.145	-5.147	.000
PO8 I understand the important issues in the relationship between people's faith and their dealings with service employees and workers (i.e. taxi drivers).		4.67				
PR9 I understand the important issues in the relationship between people's faith and their dealings with school officials / teachers	✓	3.61	-1.0	.907	-4.675	.000
PO9 I understand the important issues in the relationship between people's faith and their dealings with school officials / teachers		4.61				
PR10 I understand the important issues in the relationship between people's faith and their profession as a banker		2.72	-.500	1.150	-1.844	.083
PO10 I understand the important issues in the relationship between people's faith and their profession as a banker		3.22				
PR11 I understand the important/major issues in the relationship between people's faith and their profession as a health care professional	✓	3.94	-.778	.878	-3.757	.002
PO11 I understand the important/major issues in the relationship between people's faith and their profession as a health care professional		4.72				

Question Number	Question Content	Significant? ✓ = yes	Mean Response (1-5)	Paired sample mean difference Pre-Post	Paired Sample s.d.	t value	Significance (p=<.05)
12	PR12 I understand the important issues in the relationship between people's faith and their profession as a journalist	✓	3.67	-1.056	1.305	-3.432	.003
	PO12 I understand the important issues in the relationship between people's faith and their profession as a journalist		4.72				
13	PR13 I understand the important issues in the relationship between people's faith and their profession as an attorney		3.11	-.722	1.487	-2.060	.055
	PO13 I understand the important issues in the relationship between people's faith and their profession as an attorney		3.83				
14	PR14 I understand the important issues in the relationship between people's faith and their profession as a teacher	✓	3.50	1.000	1.085	-3.912	.001
	PO14 I understand the important issues in the relationship between people's faith and their profession as a teacher		4.50				
15	PR15 I understand the important issues in the relationship between people's faith and their work as a taxi driver	✓	2.78	1.611	.979	-6.985	.000
	PO15 I understand the important issues in the relationship between people's faith and their work as a taxi driver		4.39				
16	PR16 I believe religion it a cause of conflict in the way teachers deal with students	✓	2.94	-.889	1.491	-2.530	.022
	PO16 I believe religion it a cause of conflict in the way teachers deal with students		3.83				
17	PR17 I believe religion is a cause of conflict in the way doctors deal with patients	✓	3.28	-1.111	1.183	-3.986	..001
	PO17 I believe religion is a cause of conflict in the way doctors deal with patients		4.39				
18	PR18 I believe religion is a cause of conflict in the way lawyers deal with clients	✓	2.83	-.778	1.263	-2.613	.018
	PO18 I believe religion is a cause of conflict in the way lawyers deal with clients		3.61				

Question Number	Question Content	Significant? ✓ = yes	Mean Response (1-5)	Paired sample mean difference Pre-Post	Paired Sample s.d.	t value	Significance (p=<.05)
19	PR19 I believe religion is a cause of conflict in the way a business owner deals with employees		2.89				
	PO19 I believe religion is a cause of conflict in the way a business owner deals with employees	✓	4.11	-1.222	1.003	-5.169	.000
20	PR20 I believe religion is a cause of conflict in the way a business owner deals with the public		2.94				
	PO20 I believe religion is a cause of conflict in the way a business owner deals with the public	✓	3.94	-1.00	1.237	-3.431	.003
21	PR21 I feel adequately prepared to work as a colleague with someone from another faith		3.89				
	PO21 I feel adequately prepared to work as a colleague with someone from another faith	✓	4.61	-.722	1.364	-2.247	.038
22	PR22 I feel adequately prepared or equipped to entertain someone from another faith		3.50				
	PO22 I feel adequately prepared or equipped to entertain someone from another faith		4.17	-.667	1.455	-1.944	.069
23	PR23 I feel adequately prepared to supervise someone from another faith		3.61				
	PO23 I feel adequately prepared to supervise someone from another faith	✓	4.33	-.722	1.179	-2.600	.019
24	PR24 I feel adequately prepared to do my professional duties with clients/patients/students/customers of another faith		4.00				
	PO24 I feel adequately prepared to do my professional duties with clients/patients/students/customers of another faith		4.44	-.444	1.247	-1.512	.149
25	PR25 My professional training included (or will include) training in dealing with issues related to religion and my profession		3.28				
	PO25 My professional training included (or will include) training in dealing with issues related to religion and my profession	✓	4.22	-.944	1.514	-2.647	.017

Key:

1 = Strongly Disagree
2 = Disagree
3 = Neither Agree Nor Disagree/Not Applicable
4 = Agree
5 = Strongly Agree
6 = Not Applicable

For data analysis, we used the accepted threshold for statistical significance of a less than or equal to .05. A p value less than .01 is considered highly significant.

Endnotes

[1] The Center for Religion, the Professions and the Public was renamed the Center on Religion & the Professions in 2007.

[2] The survey was created by J. Kenneth Benson and Edward Brent, both sociologists at the University of Missouri, and commissioned by the Center on Religion & the Professions in 2003. Results have not been published.

[3] The unpublished curriculum review was done by the Center on Religion & the Professions in May 2007.

[4] The resources are housed at the Center's Web site: http://www.religionandprofessions.org.

[5] (The student who did not take either survey was not included in the analysis.) For data analysis, we used the accepted threshold for statistical significance of a less than or equal to .05, meaning that we can say with confidence that for every 100 people surveyed using our method, differences in the pre-test and post-test results could be attributed to random chance in only five of those cases. A p value less than .05 is considered an acceptable threshold for assessing significance, with significance increasing as p's value decreases. A p value less than .01 is considered highly significant. For full results of the t-tests and their corresponding p values, see the "d" appendices.

[6] The questions on which there were differences in the pre- and post-test close to significance might normally be counted, but due to the small participant size (N=18), we did not feel including these questions was justified, even if in some cases the p value was less than .03 in difference.

Section Two –
Co-curricular/Integrated Learning

Creating Interfaith and Social Justice Co-Curricular Programs

Donna McNiel, Caroline Schroeder, and
Joanna Royce-Davis
University of the Pacific

University of the Pacific's involvement with the Religion and Public Life project began in 2008 with the acceptance of our application to participate in the Institute the following summer. The Rev. Dr. Donna McNiel, University Multifaith Chaplain, Dr. Joanna Royce-Davis, Dean of Students, Dr. Caroline Schroeder, Assistant Professor, Religious and Classical Studies, and Charles Bolton, 2009 graduate and Coordinator of Interfaith Council, attended the conference in Connecticut. The opportunity to work with teams from other campuses was invaluable, not least for the sense of shared purpose in seeking to expand students' appreciation of religious exploration.

University of the Pacific, a private institution of more than 6000 students on three campuses in Northern California, provides fertile ground for the work of increasing religious literacy. Unique among institutions its size, Pacific hosts nine schools and colleges, including the School of International Studies, McGeorge School of Law, and Dugoni Dental School. Pacific is an institution that is committed to offering an educational and social environment that is inclusive and supportive of all students, faculty, staff, and alumni. These beliefs are reflected in the University's strategic directions, commitments, and values known as Pacific Rising. Included in these beliefs is the commitment to cultivate diversity, intercultural skills and global responsibility by ensuring student competencies, making diversity an integral part of curricula and student life, and creating a more diverse student body (Pacific Rising, 2007, p.5-6.) Pacific was founded as a Methodist College in 1851. While we are now non-sectarian, our heritage as a Methodist institution is an important aspect of our identity. We maintain strong connections with the United Methodist Church and the local California-Nevada Conference.

This heritage is also reflected in Pacific's commitment to individual development and whole student learning which extends to the development of students' personal and social responsibility and responsiveness to related ethical and other obligations.

Pacific benefits from its place within the diversity of the Stockton, Sacramento and San Francisco communities. The campus community echoes this diversity with no identified ethnic/racial majority group. The majority of students do identify with a particular faith tradition. Christian students make up slightly more than half of the student body. Strong Muslim, Jewish, Hindu and Sikh organizations make these traditions prominent aspects of campus life.

Faith and cultural identities are deeply intertwined for many students, staff and faculty members. And yet many assumptions about the "other" still exist, limiting the creation of an inclusive community where all members perceive being supported in their learning and success. Religious literacy is one of the critical keys to continuing to improve Pacific's campus climate, enhancing our intercultural dialogue, and creating and maintaining a more inclusive community.

In the fall of 2007, university staff were looking for tools to increase religious literacy among students in order to build a more inclusive community and to provide opportunities for both increasing self-awareness and perspective taking. Specifically, we believed that participation in the religious literacy project would allow us to purposefully scaffold and deepen the learning that is already taking place through structured intercultural dialogue, our partnerships with faith communities in the City of Stockton, and other intentionally designed learning activities.

The framework provided by Pacific's strategic plan has allowed us to create some, but not all, of the conditions necessary for the development of early religious literacy. Many of the current components of the first year experience provide opportunities for students to be introduced to religious differences and their own self-awareness of, thinking about, and experiences with religion as a whole. The first year experience at Pacific is anchored by the Pacific Seminars – a year long, common inter-disciplinary course designed to examine the question ," *What is a good Society?*" New students also participate in shared first year trips themed around social justice and sustainability, residential learning communities linked to many of the Pacific Seminar sections, and other first year programming. Building upon this foundation, we are working to develop programs that encourage students to explore their faith commitments, to learn about other faiths and social justice issues, and to practice perspective taking which will enable them to impact the world for peace and justice.

Sacred Space

Pacific has a beautiful chapel, built in 1941 to house a stunning collection of stained glass windows from a Methodist church in the Bay Area that was closing. The chapel is awe inspiring and serves our Christian community on campus well. The window designs, architecture, and furnishings of the chapel are explicitly Christian, however, and so the space does not serve the needs of students from other religious traditions, and further, reinforces the privileging of Christianity that excludes those students in various ways. We know that in order to support our diverse student body, we need to better meet their religious and spiritual needs.

In the fall of 2006 a survey of a sampling of 225 students was done to assess interest and perceived need for interfaith space. Over 40% of surveyed students said that there was a need for interfaith space, so we embarked on a long and yet to be completed process of establishing Interfaith Sacred Space. Working with partners across campus we identified a class-room in the same building as the chapel that could be made available for Sacred Space in the fall of 2009. (It is a classroom used for the first Indiana Jones movie.) We began setting aside funds to remodel the space, and the Vice President for Student Life contributed additional funds for this purpose.

The classroom, like most of the rooms in the chapel build-ing, is on a different level than the hallway leading into it. There are four steps down into the room, and a second doorway also requires going up or down stairs. We were concerned about this accessibility issue and developed several plans for address-ing the issue. However, the accessibility issues on the entire side of the building would require nearly half a million dollars to correct. So over the course of the fall we worked with physi-cal plant, the office of budget and risk management, and oth-ers to find a workable solution. The compromise was to move our heavily used bride's room to the far side of the building, away from the covered walkway, in order to establish Sacred Space in the former bride's room, adjacent to an accessible doorway and restroom. This room, too, is sunken, so a new floor was put in, thanks for $30,000 from the Vice President for Student Life, and $35,000 from the university's accessibil-ity fund.

Additionally, the Chaplain's Office was awarded an inno-vation grant in the fall of 2008 to establish an Interfaith Medi-tation Garden beside the chapel. We have met with similar challenges in overcoming resistance to doing something new, so we rejoice in incremental progress and continue working to build partnerships across campus.

Both the Sacred Space and the Interfaith Mediation Gar-den were officially opened in the fall of 2010. Sacred Space is directly across the hall from the main chapel. The student leaders of Hillel, the Muslim Student Association, and the South Asian Student Association will lead the process to furnish the large room to meet their various needs. The garden is directly out-side a side door of the chapel and will initially consist of benches and a rose garden. In future years, our student leaders will be involved in expanding this garden to include native plantings, a sustainable herb garden, and designated space for mediation or small group gatherings.

Philippines

In the Spring of 2008, we continued a campus tradition of offering a bi-annual international trip for religious exploration. Fifteen students from various disciplines, ethnic and religious backgrounds, an associate dean in Pacific's Eberhard School of Business, Dr. Ray Sylvester, a visiting Fulbright scholar, Pro-fessor Don Amorsolo, and Dr. Royce-Davis and Dr. McNiel traveled to the Philippines over spring break. We met with staff at the National Council of Churches of the Philippines and learned about their work to end the extra-judicial killings that are terrorizing the country. We spent a day at our sister school, St. Scholastica's, home of our Fulbright scholar, Professor Amorsolo. We visited the neighboring *barangay* where families live crowded into alleys along a polluted canal. St. Scholastica's seeks to develop leaders who will one day lead their communi-ties and country in overcoming such abject poverty. We trav-eled to Baguio City and met with the Rev. Pinit Penelope Caytap and learned about the indigenous communities of the Philippines and their religious, political, and social back-grounds. And we spent a day canoeing on the Pagsanjan River that ends in a magnificent trip under a waterfall.

Our group met together before, during, and after this week long trip, to learn about the social, political, and religious his-tory of the Philippines. We also explored the systems of privi-lege – racial, economic, and national – that so often divide people. And we built a community of learning. Our students were Filipino-American, Caucasian, African-American, and multi-racial. They represented a variety of academic disciplines and included both graduate and undergraduate students. Two men accompanied the thirteen women students. We were graced and challenged by encounters with new friends in the Philippines, and by the different perspectives that we all brought to the experience. We experienced culture shock – not least of all from the death defying traffic – and we relished new insights. In written feedback after the trip, every participant said that the trip had given them a deeper understanding of people whose lives are different from their own. Some of those were members of the group, and many were friends we made in Manila and Baguio City.

We are currently exploring ways to continue the relationship between Pacific and the Philippines, especially with St. Scholastica's and the Rev. Caytap. After the recent typhoons in the Philippines, our students participated in fundraisers for aid agencies in the Philippines and collected money for St. Scholastica's and their neighbors. We are also looking for ways to travel more often to the Philippines.

Sharing Daily Life

A key strategic goal is to expand residential learning community offerings to include an Interfaith and Social Justice (ISJ) community. Students have requested opportunities for deeper dialogue and relationship within and between faith and social justice groups on campus. We believed that the most direct way to do this was by "bringing it home" to the spaces where students spend most of their time and that, at least in some way, parallel the neighborhoods where they will live upon graduation. By bringing students of different faiths and perspectives on social justice together in community, we hoped to more intensely explore the Pacific Seminar question, "What is a good society?," through a number of different lenses, including religion.

In preparation for the establishment of the Interfaith and Social Justice Residential Learning Community, we sought to develop a model for ongoing dialogue that would be centered upon daily life. We thought that this might include dinner time panel discussions, shared and interpreted celebrations of religious holidays, explorations of household customs among religious traditions, as well as shared outreach experiences and other opportunities. We planned to introduce these aspects to the Chapel's programming in the prior academic year in preparation for the establishment of the residential program the following year.

During the meeting of the Institute in the summer of 2008, we fine tuned our plan for the community. A key adjustment was the inclusion of "Social Justice" in the community's title and orientation. We wanted to intentionally invite students into the community who might not identify with a particular religious tradition, but who shared an interest in learning about religious traditions and working on issues that cut across religious differences.

Dr. Schroeder volunteered to teach a focused section of Pacific Seminar 1, the introductory first year course that would include members of the Interfaith and Social Justice learning community. We hoped this would help to deepen relationships among the community members and allow their conversations to flow more easily between classroom and residence hall. We identified aspects of the Resident Advisor and Student Advisors programs that could help foster the core goals of building inclusive community, exploring differences, and gaining self-awareness among members of the community.

During the 2008-2009 academic year the team met with Housing and Greek Life Staff to identify appropriate space for this community, in the residence hall closest to the chapel. We prepared flyers and information for the spring housing brochure. We talked with potential residents during the spring preview day for high school seniors who had been accepted to Pacific. We worked with Student Support Services to ensure that residents in the community would be assigned to Dr. Schroeder's section of Pacific Seminar. We identified a student advisor, Ashton Datcher, who was excited about the program. And we met with the Resident Advisor, Chinwe Ohanele, who chose to work with the Interfaith & Social Justice Community.

It seemed that the key pieces were in place as new student orientation began in June. Our goal was to recruit six to twelve entering students for the Interfaith & Social Justice (ISJ) Residential Learning Community. Due to unexpected limited housing availability and related factors (including a larger than normal entering class, student roommate preferences, and the reassignment of the designated Student Advisor to another floor), introduction of the ISJ community was piloted with two students. During 2010, 15 students participated in the residential learning community, and programming was expanded to involve area scholars and faith leaders. The majority of students who expressed an interest in the community, or in our faith and justice organizations enrolled in Dr. Schroeder's section of Pacific Seminar. This has contributed to closer relationships among these students, especially the students living in the area of the planned learning community.

The course is a university-wide requirement for all incoming first-year students, and twenty-one attended Dr. Schroeder's section. The syllabus and textbook (which Dr. Schroeder co-desiged and coedited) are organized into five units: The Self and Self-Reflection, Family and Interpersonal Relationships, Civil Society, Citizenship and the State, and The Natural World and the Environment. Each of the units contained readings, which related to the themes of social justice or religion. The Buddhist texts *Dhammapada* and the Four Noble Truths were in unit 1, along with three readings on racial identity and stereotyping. In unit two, students read an essay by Carter Heyward, a lesbian priest, about coming out and the way her religious faith empowers her sexuality and her public work. In Unit Three, students read an essay by Diana Eck on religious pluralism. Unit four contained *Antigone*, which deals with religious commitments, as well as a variety of essays on citizenship addressing multiple social justice issues (race and citizenship, national and international civil rights, gays in the military, and marriage equality). Finally in Unit Five were two readings about religion or spirituality and nature by John Muir and Leslie Marmo Silko as well as an article about environmental racism. The course also assigned two movies that were broadcast on the closed circuit campus television station: *The Namesake* (based on the book by Jhumpa Lahiri) and the documentary *Murderball*. We hosted viewings of these movies in the residence hall with pizza and refreshments. This shared experience reinforces the ties between classroom and campus life, and supports the relationships among students in the residence hall. Dr. Schroeder then led discussions of the films in the seminar class.

As students progressed through the course, they made noticeable developments in understanding the roles of both the individual and the larger society in creating and addressing issues of social inequality. They also discussed how individual religious commitments or religious knowledge can productively contribute to society and can be used to weaken the fabric of social and civic bonds in society. Many students chose to write their papers focusing on texts and issues related to religion, diversity, or social justice.

Learning Curve

During the inaugural semester of the residential community, we have become aware of the need to clarify priorities in the housing assignment process, and to be clear about those priorities with new and returning students. Future plans include recruiting returning students to join the community for the coming academic year in order to "anchor" the community and help reserve rooms in the residence hall. The programming of the residential community has been much more dependent upon the Resident Advisor and Student Advisor than anticipated. This requires close coordination with these student leaders to help develop programming that connects to the work students are doing in Pacific Seminar.

The first year of the residential learning community was frustrating in many ways. It has also been critically important, not only for the ISJ community, but for the future of all of Pacific's residential learning communities as the Division of Student Life seeks to clarify our goals in student housing, particularly for first year students, and our priorities in residence life programming.

Pushing On

These efforts are all designed to encourage lasting relationships among our students and to support their practice and exploration of the variety of faith traditions that they represent. We work to discover the many things we all hold in common, and to celebrate the ways in which we differ. Those differences are each person's unique contribution to the Pacific community, and to the communities in which our students live and work when they graduate from Pacific. Our diverse community presents many challenges, and countless opportunities for exploration, growth, and inspiration. We are participating in the formation of leaders who will reach across dividing differences in creative and exciting ways. In order to do that, we must be continually pushing against the boundaries that keep us stuck in old ways of being and do not serve all of our students. Fortunately, Pacific is succeeding in this, step by incremental step.

References

Pacific Rising, 2008 – 2015. (2007) Retrieved January 12, 2010, from University of Pacific website: http://www.pacific.edu/Documents/provost/acrobat/pacific_rising.pdf

Human Moral Development Living Learning Community: A Brief Biography

Eric Thurman
Sewanee: The University of the South

Institutional Context

Sewanee, the University of the South, according to our university purpose statement, is dedicated to the process of self assessment within the framework of critical thinking, acceptance and regard for others. In light of this commitment to self-examination and communal inquiry, we believe it necessary for students to reflect on the process of their moral development from multiple disciplinary perspectives. We imagine our respective disciplinary interests to be more like friendly conversation partners, rather than rival claimants to intellectual authority in this endeavor. Anthropology brings a focus on practice and cultural diversity that might be juxtaposed with the abstract reflection on the basic concerns of all human beings that is characteristic of philosophy. Both can inform the study of religion, which in turn might pose further questions about how traditions related to "the sacred" both shape and are shaped by the history of human practices and intellectual reflection. Our project thus aims at providing students with the opportunity of engaging significant questions of moral value and reasoning through the establishment of the Human Moral Development Living Learning Community (LLC).

Sewanee, "the only university in the nation that is owned and governed by dioceses of the Episcopal Church," (An Episcopal University, para. 1) is a four-year university with around 1400 students who pursue some 36 majors, 27 minors, and 15 special programs in the liberal arts and natural and social sciences (About Sewanee, para. 2). Part of Sewanee's First Year Experience, LLCs are theme-based resident programs that aim to connect students and faculty advisors in areas of shared intellectual interest. To sign up for an LLC, first year students choose from a pre-selected list of courses connected to the LLC theme and taught by participating faculty during the Fall semester. Each LLC consists of anywhere from 21-35 first-year students, 3 to 4 upper class Assistant Proctors (APs) who live with those students, and a team of 3 to 4 faculty advisors from different departments. Working together, the members of an LLC plan and engage in co-curricular activities that are intended to complement classroom learning: community projects, field trips, lecture series, leadership training, and informal conversation over shared meals. LLCs are meant to foster closer relationships between faculty and students, promote student leadership, and bridge the gap between academic and residential life on campus.

Our LLC was one of eight operating during the 2009-2010 academic year, the second year of the LLC program at Sewanee. Since the faculty involved had changed from the time of the SVHE Institute on Religion in the summer of 2008, the initial focus and scope of the LLC was changed as well. Noting where our respective disciplines might best overlap, the new faculty team broadened its interests from a community focused specifically on religion, culture, and identity to one with a focus on multiple dimensions of personal moral development. Consequently, any discussion of religious literacy would be part of a more robust interdisciplinary conversation, a fitting framework for exploring these issues at a liberal arts institution like Sewanee.

Beginnings

Our Human Moral Development LLC is committed to examining the "values held by various societies and cultures and engages students in their own process of decision-making and discernment, leading ultimately to informed engagement with the Sewanee and world communities." (Human Moral Development). The interdisciplinary dimension of that commitment is evident from the courses we offered to the 18 first-year students who signed up for the LCC in the summer of 2009: Introduction to Anthropology (ANTH); Chinese Philosophy (PHIL); The Ethics of Honor (PHIL); and Introduction to Religion (REL). Our LLC only came to life, however, once students arrived on campus in late August. On the first day of New Student Orientation week, our advisees initially met with their APs. Later that same day, the students had their first meeting with us as advisors. We deliberately added additional, informal meetings of the entire LLC in the weeks to follow in order to welcome everyone and begin to think about our goals and how we would reach them this year.

Ideally, the activities and direction of LLCs are driven by student interests and initiative. Faculty are meant to advise and facilitate, while logistics are handled by the Department of Resident Life through the designated (and invaluable) LLC Coordinator. Though we agreed with this model in principle, we also anticipated the difficulty a group of first-year students new to the community and college life might face in imagining viable projects. When a member of our faculty team learned early in the semester of a potential project from his community contacts, we thus agreed to present the idea to the students as our main activity for the term. The project would involve students assisting with a day-long workshop on parenting and childcare for new mothers sponsored by the Health Department of a neighboring county with a high number of families living in poverty. Our students would lead three workshops on reading to children in an effort to encourage the practice at home. Our hope was that through their work the students might begin to reflect on the moral issues raised by the relationship between economics and early childhood education.

Planning began in earnest soon after a majority of students agreed to participate in the project, which was scheduled for early October. We invited the Health Department director to discuss the details and goals of the workshop and a specialist from the University offered pedagogical advice on how to talk to new mothers about reading to children. In the weeks leading up to the workshop, students formed teams and developed their own approaches to presenting the workshop material. On the day of the workshop, students lead their "Ready, Set, "Read" sessions, while faculty observed and participated in group discussions. Many students also volunteered for other tasks at the event location such as supervising children, handing out snacks, and assisting visitors with directions.

Initial Reflections

To date, most of our assessment efforts have been informal. We intend, however, to implement more formal tools at the beginning of the Spring semester and again at the end of the year. Mid-year efforts will involve an anonymous survey requesting written responses to four, open-ended questions: (1) what have you enjoyed most about participating in this LLC? (2) what have you enjoyed least about participating in this LCC? (3) what can you do to make your participation more meaningful? (4) what can we as faculty and student leaders do to make participation more meaningful? End of the year assessment may include the same survey as well as an additional summary group conversation or further written responses.

With respect to our main semester project, our initial impression as faculty advisors was that the workshops were a success. Those of us who attended the event noted that the students were able effectively to communicate their information and engage visitors and their concerns. Informal conversations with students who participated also confirmed that most students found their preparation and interaction both informative and rewarding. Many students were not previously aware of the disparities in wealth that exist between Sewanee and many of the surrounding communities. Nor were they aware of what they might be abe to do to address the effects of that situation. After the event, however, several students expressed an interest in finding or developing other, similar outreach opportunities in light of their experience in the workshop.

With around 50% student participation in this event (and other informal meetings), we are both surprised and pleased at the energy and momentum of the LLC. Perhaps the most important challenges we have faced so far are developing leaders from among the first year students and integrating the issues raised by our co-curricular activities into our classroom experiences. We as faculty faced significant challenges in successfully incorporating additional moral topics into our syllabi in a way that contributed to our course goals. Interdisciplinary possibilities abound for thinking about the complex relationship between family income, informal education, and personal moral development. Yet actualizing those possibilities meaningfully proved difficult for most of us. We imagine that this kind of integration will become easier as we continue to talk and plan together.

Developing student leaders has been more quickly remedied. One member of our faculty team suggested the students form a steering committee within the LLC community. This committee would then be responsible for taking the initiative in any further planning. From that suggestion one first-year student has stepped up as the leader of the committee. She has culled together other first-year students and coordinated with faculty to come up with the plans that will guide our Spring semester. At the time of writing, the committee plans to present three possible projects to the entire LLC for their consideration. Needless to say, we are eager to hear about those plans and happy to see students now guiding the direction of the community.

Overall, our LLC has begun to achieve many of the goals set for LCCs in general at Sewanee. Each of us has commented on the benefits to having our advisees as students in our classes during that crucial first semester. We interact with our students in more than one context and so can better asses their personalities and learning styles; the students in turn are more comfortable with us as advisors, and are hopefully more willing to listen to the advice we offer about course selection and academic life in general. Ideally, we model for them what it looks like to be intellectually engaged in the world around us, as one of our team members points out, and that might be the single most important, if immeasurable, difference the LLCs make. Each of us has also commented on how participation in the LLC affects student relationships. Most students seem to appreciate having a ready-made, if-not-fully-formed community to which they immediately belong their first year. We have noticed positive relationships develop in our LLC beyond the initial advising groups and we have identified several students who have shown clear leadership potential. It is perhaps no coincidence that initial data from the Dean of Student Life shows that students in LLCs at Sewanee have higher GPAs and lower numbers of disciplinary incidents than their peers not in LLCs.

Looking Back, Looking Ahead

Since we are in the middle of our first year with our LLC, we are still very much in the process of absorbing the experience. For newer faculty members on the team, learning to think and act on an ad-hoc basis has been particularly helpful, as has the additional opportunity to work with students outside of the classroom. We have all learned even more to value interdisciplinary conversations, while at the same time coming to better appreciate the time and effort needed for incorporating those conversations in the classroom. If there is any advice we might give to institutions planning interdisciplinary LLCs like ours, it might be to make sure there is adequate support for integrating co-curricular activities with the curricular objectives of specific classes. Preparation time to define adequately the goals of the LLCs *and* make adjustments to existing course syllabi is key to combining group engagement with personal reflection.

As noted above, the initial plans for this LLC were changed from the blue-print drawn up at the SVHE's Institute on Religion in Curriculum and Culture in the summer of 2008. By providing time and the opportunity for extended dialogue about what an LLC could be, the leaders and participants at the Institute nevertheless helped make its present incarnation possible. Most informative were the conversations we had with our small-group leaders who encouraged us to think more broadly than we otherwise might have. Most inspiring were the stories and plans of other participating institutions. Listening to the specific challenges other groups faced and seeing their determined plans to meet those challenges with creativity and passion did much to help us overcome our own hesitations.

Though the future of our Human Moral Development LLC's future is tied up in part with the existence of the LLC program at Sewanee, current signs point to both continuing as part of the First Year Experience. As we begin a new semester with our LLC, we look forward to the projects our students will engage. Our hope is to plan more time for reflecting on their experiences by sharing what human moral development means to us in light of our different disciplinary training. Whatever the future of our LLC and the LLC program itself, we all, faculty and students, look forward to living and learning — together.

References

About Sewanee. Retrieved March 9, 2010 from Sewanee the University of the South website at: http://about.sewanee.edu/

An Episcopal University. Retrieved March 9, 2010 from Sewanee the University of the South website at: http://about.sewanee.edu/episcopal

Human Moral Development. *Course Information for the Class of 2013*. Retrieved March 9, 2010 from Sewanee the University of the South website at: http://sitemason.sewanee.edu/files/fIoXxm/Course%20Information%20for%20the%20Class%20of%202013.pdf

Learning Communities. Retrieved March 9, 2010 from Sewanee the University of the South website at http://www2.sewanee.edu/sewaneescene/LC

University Purpose. Retrieved March 9, 2010 from Sewanee the University of the South website at: http://about.sewanee.edu/purpose

Thanks go to the following people: Richard O'Connor and Jim Peterman for their work as faculty leaders; Grace Greenwell, Carrie Ryan, and Luca Koritsanszky for their work as student APs; and Jim Pappas for his work as LLC Coordinator. Though the views expressed here were informed in different ways by each of these individuals, I alone am responsible for the content of this essay.

Section Three –

University-Wide/ Interdisciplinary Programs

Monotheistic Religions and the Public Square

Thomas D. Kennedy, Michael Bailey, and Brian Carroll
Berry College

Berry College is a private liberal arts college located in Rome, Georgia. Founded by Martha Berry in 1902 as an industrial school for under-privileged boys, Berry College graduated its first class in 1932. Although never related to a particular church, the college whose motto is "Not to be ministered unto, but to minister," to this day describes itself as a "comprehensive liberal arts college with Christian values." The student body self-identifies as heavily Protestant, and although there is only the standard curricular attention to religion and philosophy of a liberal arts college, there is a very lively extra-curricular program in Christian activities as well as an active interfaith center.

Given the character of the institution, we had multiple aims in developing our project. Despite the self-identification of the large number of our students as from a broad range of evangelical Christian backgrounds, our experience was that these students knew less about their own faith tradition—its texts, its rituals and practices, its theology and its ethics—and a whole lot less about other faiths than they supposed. Our goal was to help these students to have a more nuanced and sophisticated understanding of the Christian tradition and the various ways Christian thinkers have understood their faith as playing a role in political decision-making. Other Berry College students are secular. We would like these students to think more carefully and respectfully about religious identity and how a democracy might respect discrete identities. We would like all our students to understand the complexity not only of their own tradition (or lack of tradition) but also of other religious faiths and traditions, in particular Judaism and Islam, and we believe a course that we envision could be very valuable to this end.

Initially, our goal was to construct a course (and perhaps, as well, to construct units for other courses in philosophy and religion, government, and communications) the focus of which would be an examination of perspectives (and the range of perspectives) within Judaism, Christianity, and Islam on the relevance of one's faith to political decision-making in a democratic context like ours. How do various "people of the book" understand the relevance of "the book" to political life in democratic societies? We hope in our course to identify common ground as well as to explore real differences in our attempt to answer the question as citizens of a democracy and, perhaps, also as religious believers, "How naked should the public square be in a pluralistic society?" Our core concern is to offer students (most of whom are religiously serious) an opportunity to think more rigorously about their own faith and to receive an introduction to the moral and political thought of Judaism and Islam as the students reflect upon their own roles as citizens in a pluralistic democracy. For a number of reasons, chief among them the national economic downturn, our project morphed into three to four discrete projects. Rather than one interdisciplinary course, at least three disciplinary courses were substantially impacted by this work and we have material on hand for a fourth disciplinary/interdisciplinary course in the future.

Professor Michael Bailey of the Department of Government teaches two departmental courses that have been transformed by our conversations at the Institute: a capstone course for majors that explores how religion is understood by the discipline of political science and a *Religion and Politics in the United States* course. The primary goal of the latter course is to provide students with the information and analytical tools to understand and critically evaluate the relationship between politics and religion in the United States. In this class, students examine key conflicts between the two disciplines over several periods of American history. They study how the First Amendment has informed interactions between religion and politics over time, as well as the role of Christianity and other faiths in American governance.

Assignments include weekly response papers and essays, in addition to mid-term and final examinations. (See Appendix for an excerpted course syllabus.) Students in this class have made great progress in: (a) appreciating the bewilderingly complex relationship between religion and politics, (b) understanding how disagreements over religion have led to a wide range of political controversies and disputes; (c) recognizing the impossibility of attaining a perfectly neutral political stance toward religion.

Another course directly impacted by Berry's participation in the Institute was Professor Brian Carroll's Honors/Communication *Freedom of Expression®* class, which includes a large section on religious expression, religious freedoms, and pluralism in America. Recommended readings for the class include *Christianity and American Democracy* by Hugh Heclo and colleagues (Harvard University, 2009) and *Religious Freedom and the Constitution,* Christopher Eisgruber & Lawrence G. Sager (Harvard University, 2007). For the course capstone project, students are asked to consider means of expressing views on a matter of public policy of their own choosing, and write a paper evaluating how their mode of expression intersects with First Amendment principles.

At the Institute, the team worked on and discussed the course at length with a diverse and accomplished roster of professors from throughout the country.

Finally, although Dean Kennedy's *Introduction to Christian Ethics* course was somewhat altered through his participation in the Institute, the greater influence of the Institute has been upon a course he is currently developing on monotheistic religions and war. The course will open with an introductory unit on Judaism, Christianity, and Islam—the unit on Islam having been contributed by Adam Gaiser and the Florida State University team at the Institute. A key concern in this first section is the various understandings of sources for ethical reflection in the three traditions, and conceptions of moral norms and the divine law. Following this, students will examine each of these traditions and their understandings of just(ified) war and pacifism. The benefits of the Institute and our project, have been immense for faculty at Berry College and that has surely been one of the greatest successes of the project for us. Three well-trained academics were granted the leisure time to discuss and develop a course of significant import and were assisted in this with the counsel of other experienced colleagues. That, in itself, has been immensely worthwhile and our ongoing conversations have been among the greatest successes of the project. Other successes, of course, include the enriching of our individual courses.

The greatest challenges in implementing the course to this point have resulted from the economic downturn. In a nutshell, we are trying to do more with less, and that means considerably less freedom to deliver a team-taught course. As things return to normal, we hope that we will have the opportunity to deliver some version of the course that we conceived together. In the meantime, we have the 3-4 independent courses that have been re-visioned due to our project work.

The Society for Values in Higher Education Institute on Religion in Curriculum and Culture was immensely valuable for us in certain respects, primarily in providing Professors Bailey, Carroll, and Kennedy with the leisure to reflect and discuss (in a lovely setting with some really amazing food) matters of great national and curricular import. Another significant benefit was the opportunity to meet fellow academics from other institutions with similar interests and experiences and to learn from them. The range of academic interests and specializations on various teams was most impressive and the informal interdisciplinary conversation opportunities were greatly enriching.

It is certainly our hope that our interests will lead to continuing conversations and curricular collaboration in the future. We are wonderfully different, but we share the conviction that religious illiteracy is a problem at Berry, as well as a learning opportunity. A new course for the Honors Program could promote democratic citizenship by religiously literate citizens, and could help Berry students better understand their own faiths as well as other faiths held by fellow citizens.

Appendix

Course Syllabus (Excerpted)

GOV 450 Religion and Politics in the United States

Spring 2009

Michael E. Bailey   TTH: 2:00-3:30

Course Description: This course explores the relationship between politics and religion. Because the subject is far too large to examine comprehensively in the span of a semester, our exploration is necessarily selective. One such limitation is that we focus most of our time on how religion plays out politically in the American regime. A second limitation is that we will deal predominantly, though by no means exclusively, with how defenders of the Christian faith have grappled with articulating the role of religion in the public square.

Readings:
- Wills, G. (2007) *Head and Heart: American Christianities* (New York: Penguin Press)
- Kemeny, P.C.(Ed.) (2007) *Church, State and Public Justice: Five Views* (Downers Grove, IL: IVP Academic)
- Waldman, S. (2009) *Founding Faith: How Our Founding Fathers Forged a Radical New Approach to Religious Liberty* (New York: Random House)
- Wald, K. D. (2003) *Religion and Politics in the United States* (Lanham, MD: Rowman & Littlefield)
- Handouts

Purpose:
The purpose of this course is for students to examine and better understand the complicated, troubling and varied relationship between politics and religion in the United States—both in its contemporary and historical manifestations. The relationship between politics and religion is not, to understate

the case, a simple one. Both the church and the state argue for their own sovereign authority, and each has a tendency to fit all human affairs within their respective spheres. Complicating matters is that (a) most religious texts, including the Bible, are not works of systematic political theory, and (b) the Constitution's stance toward religion in the public sphere is ambiguous. As a result, not only do the irreligious and religious do political battle with one another, but committed believers disagree strongly with one another on nearly every imaginable political point. This course is designed to examine a number of these points disagreements as they have played out over time in the American context as well as to discover, where possible, where there exists points of principled agreement.

Student Learning outcomes:

The primary goal of the course is to provide students with the information and analytical tools to understand and critically evaluate the relationship between politics and religion in the United States. Specifically:

- You will demonstrate that you understand the fundamental concepts crucial to an informed discussion of the relationship between religion in politics in the United States.
- You will demonstrate knowledge of the battles that shaped politics and religion with respect to but not limited to:
    The Puritans
    The Founding period
    The Civil Rights movement
    And contemporary politics.
- You will demonstrate knowledge of the relationship of religion and politics as it connects to the 1st Amendment, both at the time of its formation as well as its being informed by the Supreme Court over the last fifty years.
- You will demonstrate an understanding of how disparate Christian perspectives have formulated competing understandings of the proper relationship of religion and politics.
- You will demonstrate the changing historical role and influence of religious minorities in American politics.

Assessment Measures:
- You will demonstrate satisfactory knowledge of the afore-mentioned topics through an essays, exams, and weekly journals.

Assignments:

20% of grade: Mid-term exam.

20% of grade: Final exam.

40% of grade: Two essays. (20% each).

10% of grade: 10 weekly response papers of about 1-2 pages (about 400 words) for the first 10 weeks.

>5%: Attendance.

5%: Participation.

Schedule of Lecture Topics

Introduction
   Overview and basic terms

UNIT ONE: HISTORY OF RELIGION AND POLITICS IN THE U.S.
Puritanism and other early religious influences
Religion and the Founding Fathers
      Enlightenment
      Founding Faith, the Constitution, and 1st Amendment
19th Century religion in the United States
20th Century religion in the United States

UNIT TWO: CONTEMPORARY RELIGION AND POLITICS IN THE U.S.
      Competing Contemporary Christian views of Church and State
      Introduction of the five views
      Responses
Religion and the Court today:
      Establishment Clause
      Liberal neutrality?
      Free Exercise Clause
Religious minorities in the United States today
How evangelical is United States politics?
      Public opinion
      Evangelicalism

Responsible Belief: Students in a pervasively-Christian university engaging in interfaith dialogue

Marion H. Larson, Julia Moen,
and Sara L. H. Shady
Bethel University

In *Acts of Faith*, Eboo Patel, founder and director of the Interfaith Youth Core, suggests that "the twenty-first century will be shaped by the question of the faith line" (p. xv). He goes on to defend a form of religious pluralism "that affirms the identity of the constituent communities while emphasizing that the well-being of each and all depends on the health of the whole" (2007. p. xv). This approach places an emphasis on the need for open dialogue between persons from different traditions that enables them to learn from, and even experience, each other's perspective. Given the reality of the "faith line," the need for interreligious dialogue is obvious.

Some college and university campuses aren't doing much to promote interreligious dialogue because too many on their campus question the appropriateness of academic institutions bringing religion into the picture at all. On other campuses, growing numbers of student life personnel and faculty are suggesting that there may be a place for considerations of religious issues in the academy. (In 2008, Oxford University Press released a collection of articles edited by Douglas Jacobsen and Rhonda Hustedt Jacobsen entitled *The American University in a Postsecular Age* which provides support for such a claim, while also considering some of the issues that such a move might raise.)

For many faith-based colleges and universities, however, the idea that religious issues and perspectives should be considered in the classroom isn't new. On the contrary! For example, at Bethel University (a Baptist-affiliated institution, where faculty and a significant majority of students consider themselves evangelical Christians), we seek to educate students holistically—looking for ways to connect their experiences in the dorm, in field practicum and service projects, or in chapel with their classroom learning, and vice versa. Faith-based institutions like Bethel consider "integration of faith and learning" as central to this holistic education, and faculty work hard to help students consider how their faith commitments might influence their approaches to their academic learning, as well as how their academic learning might affect their faith.

As part of Bethel's general education curriculum, all students are required to take two courses in biblical studies and one in Christian theology. In addition, many other courses in general education (such as those in the arts and humanities or in the sciences) as well as at least some courses in each major directly address the implications of Christian belief and practice for considering significant questions of human existence. Further, our students are exposed to ways in which Christians in the past—both Protestant and Catholic—have thought and acted, both for good and for ill. The capstone seminar in our general education curriculum is one in which seniors consider together what it might mean to be persons of faith seeking to bring our beliefs to bear on various contemporary issues they may face upon graduation.

Our students, then, have ample opportunities to approach Christianity as both a subject for academic study and as a foundation for a growing and vibrant spirituality. They study with faculty and peers who "take religion seriously." To "take religion seriously," says Warren Nord, students must study a "living religious tradition in some depth" and be encouraged to be "open to the possibility that religious categories provide credible ways of making sense of the world," seeing religion as a "live option" even for thinking people living in the 21st century (2008, p.167).

Bethel students learn to take Christianity seriously, but they receive very little exposure to the faith traditions and beliefs of other religions. While they are required to take general education courses in world cultures and second languages, these courses do not necessarily address religious literacy or religious diversity. Our students may be fluent speakers of "Christian," but we want our project to spark campus efforts to help increasing numbers of our students become "theologically bilingual, to understand the God-language of another community, and to understand our own more clearly in the process" (Eck, 2003, p. xvi). This involves both intellectual and experiential learning.

When we started talking more seriously about how we might engage our students with others across faith lines, we realized that we had much to learn from those whose more diverse campus environments gave them experiences in this area. The Religion and Public Life Project seemed like an ideal opportunity for us to interact with faculty and administrators from various institutions, to learn from the project facilitators, and to spend time together as a team off campus.

Our primary goal for the Religion and Public Life project was to provide opportunities and tools for peer-peer interfaith dialogue in order to promote understanding of self and other. More specifically, our learning outcomes on an intellectual level were for students to:

- Deepen their understanding of their own Christian faith tradition
- Understand how their own Christian knowledge and experience fits within the context of other Christian faith traditions

- See ways in which people of various faiths have much in common
- Recognize that each religion has varied expressions

As a result of their involvement, we wanted students to value:
- Critiques of Christianity offered by proponents of other religions
- The religious experiences of others
- Their own religious beliefs and experiences
- On a skill-based level, we hoped students would gain the ability to:
- Use tools of moral conversation
- Critically discuss religion and religious issues
- Use research and evaluation tools to find credible information about religious topics

Our target population for the religion and public life project was students in the following courses:
- First-year students in our Honors Program (26 students began the Honors Program in Fall 2008 and thus took a required course for incoming first-year students in called "Meaning and Persons")
- Sophomore-junior students enrolled in an upper-level course for Philosophy majors "Social and Political Philosophy" (9 students took the course in the Fall of 2008)
- Social Work majors enrolled in Social Work Field Instruction (a senior-level professional course with 20 students)

We decided to start with students in these courses because as the instructors of these courses, we have some control over the curriculum and, hence, the requirements for students; the subject matter and goals for these courses makes them logical sites for connecting with interfaith dialogue; and we wanted to expose students from a range of majors and at both first-year and upper-class levels to interfaith dialogue, thus giving us a good sense of how successful we might be in the future as we seek to encourage more students to get off campus and interact with people across faith lines.

Each faculty member developed a course-appropriate opportunity for students in these classes to engage in interfaith dialogue and reflection.

Marion Larson had students in her first-term Honors class learn more about a faith tradition that isn't their own and then write a series of short papers reflecting on this project. In the class, students read books featuring characters who are in search of meaning in their lives, whose journey often takes them to (or away from) a particular religious community. Students were asked to learn more about an unfamiliar religious tradition, and reflect on this process. Students could choose to complete this project through library research, through attending interfaith dialogue sessions sponsored by the St. Paul Interfaith Network, or a combination of the two.

Sara Shady had students in her upper-level social and political philosophy class consider the role of religion and religious pluralism in society. As part of this consideration, all students read material about the role of religion in civil society in a religiously pluralistic society and discussed it in class. Their final term paper required students to explore, analyze and evaluate a topic related to the role of religion in contemporary society, given the rise of religious diversity in the West. Students could choose to attend interfaith dialogue sessions sponsored by the St. Paul Interfaith Network as part of their research for this project.

Julia Moen had students in their social work practicum experiences reflect on questions related to religion and their work with clients. As a core competency in the professional program, students learn to "engage diversity and difference in practice." In their field practicum site, students were asked to learn about a religious tradition different from their own. They wrote journal entries reflecting on their religious literacy, commonality and differences between religious traditions, and the ways in which religious diversity influences their work with colleagues and clients.

The three faculty met several times and have interacted with selected students who participated in these opportunities so that we can learn what worked well and what might be improved in the future.

In addition, each of us has met with faculty and staff in

various areas on campus (including student life) to learn about others who are also working to increase students' abilities to make connections and begin to form relationships across faith lines. We have attended on-campus Interreligious Symposia sponsored by faculty in Religious Studies, and we have continued to be involved with the St. Paul Interfaith Network. In Fall 2009, Sara Shady once again had students in the "Meaning and Persons" Honors class participate in off-campus interfaith dialogues.

We plan to continue looking for ways in which we might make course-appropriate connections with interfaith dialogue opportunities off campus, thereby encouraging more students to participate and helping them process the challenges some of them feel when they do so. In addition, we hope to build a larger group of faculty and student life staff who will support such efforts.

The primary means of assessing learning outcomes has been through the writing we have assigned to our students. In each case, we've had students reflect deliberately on connections, questions, and challenges they have noted through their interactions with other faith traditions.

Meaning and Persons: In this class, students read a novel and two memoirs that address issues of spirituality and religious identity. Class discussion of these materials helped lay the groundwork for their larger "Learn to Listen" project. In this project, students were to collect information about a faith tradition other than their own, present this information as clearly as they could, reflect on ways in which they found connections between this tradition and their own beliefs and spiritual practices, and reflect on ways in which they felt disconnected from or had questions about this tradition. Although students were given the option of completing this assignment through library research, they were strongly encouraged to participate in the interfaith dialogue series sponsored by a local interfaith network. (See the appended assignment sheet that students were given, as well as a more full description of the interfaith dialogue series, "My Truth and Your Truth.")

Social and Political Philosophy: Student understanding of course readings related to the role of religion in civil society within a pluralist democracy was assessed through class discussions and a take home essay exam. Students then chose a focus area within this topic to explore in their final paper, and researched their final papers through both academic research and participation in the interfaith dialogue series.

Social Work Field Instruction: Student knowledge of religious diversity in their work with clients and colleagues was assessed through a journal writing project. Students did a self-assessment based on the questions they were asked to reflect on and faculty assessed student journals using a Delphi method and coded responses to understand student knowledge and skills on religious diversity for the purpose of needed program and curriculum development.

Our work (so far)has focused primarily on increasing students' interactions with people from other faiths, rather than on gaining knowledge about a particular faith tradition. Of course these interactions have helped students learn more about other faith traditions, but most of our students are not any more likely now to be able to state the major tenets of, say, Islam or Judaism. They did, however, come to "see ways in which people of various faiths have much in common" and "recognize that each religion has varied expressions," two of our knowledge-based outcomes.

It makes sense that their interaction with others through the interfaith dialogues would lead to such outcomes. A Protestant Christian can't help but feel connections with a Muslim speaker who talks about his desire to follow God faithfully, with a Jewish discussion partner who shares the profound spiritual questions she still asks in the wake of the Holocaust, or with a Catholic priest who talks about his understanding of God's grace. One said, "It was surprising to find myself agreeing with many statements [made by other participants], even seeing how similar some traditions are to my own Christian faith." Several remarked that they were humbled by the "dedication and reverence" with which those from other faith traditions approached God. Others noted that Christians need to learn from Muslims to cultivate the "strong sense of community," one that includes even "constant accountability." One student said: "Christians could definitely learn about commitment to their religious views and living out what they believe from Muslim people." Particularly for those students who are deeply convinced of the rightness (and even superiority) of their own religion, it's remarkable that several came to see not only similarities between religions but even ways in which Christian practice may be inadequate.

Their knowledge of the "varied expressions" within different religious traditions came in a place that surprised many of them—within Christianity itself. Students at our institution are overwhelmingly Protestant and theologically conservative. Because so many of their conversations about religion occur on campus with each other, it becomes easy for them to come to assume that "all Christians" think or act as they do. The interfaith dialogues in which they participated, though, helped them see that this is not the case. Although believers in several religious and spiritual traditions (including Judaism, Islam, Baha'i, Hinduism, and both Protestant and Catholic Christianity) participated in these dialogues, the majority of those in attendance practice Christianity in some form. Other than our students, however, few evangelical Protestants attended. This meant that most discussion tables included several Christian participants, which led our students to expect that they would agree on most matters. When that proved not to be the case, some were "frustrated at how [those]…who claim to be Christians adhere to postmodern thought or extreme religious pluralism." Others felt that some participants tried to "twist Christianity to seem more appealing." This led one student to say that he felt that "the goal of these dialogues was to point out faults in Christianity and to get Christians to reconsider their views." More accurately, though, it should be said that these dialogues challenged those with exclusivist religious views to reconsider their perspective, often through simple exposure to committed believers of other faith traditions.

Because most of our students chose to participate in off-campus interfaith dialogues, the outcomes that their writing reflected most strongly had to do with what they came to value. In particular, the reflections of several indicated that they began learning to "take seriously the critiques of Christianity offered by proponents of other religions," "value the religious experiences of others," and "value their own religious beliefs and experiences," the three value-focused outcomes we had identified for our project. Several expressed their overall reactions to the interfaith dialogue in very positive terms, saying that they felt closer to God, "on a 'religious high'" as a result of "discussing my faith with people of different faiths." Even those who felt somewhat embattled by the "many expressions of postmodern religion at these dialogues" noted that the experience inspired them to want to take their own faith more seriously. As one said, "I am just another human being among the millions, who is yearning to know truth and live it. It is a humbling, awakening realization. I thank God for this opportunity to be so deeply challenged."

In assessing student learning based on social work journal entries, most notable were six students who had participated in a study abroad semester program. One of those students wrote, "Learning about Hinduism in India was unexpectedly valuable in my ability to understand and relate to the clients. Even in staff meeting today, we were talking about the fear of refugee elders who are unsure of dying in non-Hindu culture and country because of what would happen to their bodies. I was able to share with staff my knowledge about death in Hinduism and reasons why they might be fearful. Knowledge of Hinduism helped me build trust and confidence with my clients. I love to learn how faith shapes the everyday lives and purpose of my clients and co-workers." The journal assignment provided an opportunity to assess the knowledge and skills of interfaith relationships with a cohort of students. One outcome is a proposed change in course objectives at the introductory level (sophomore year) to junior and senior year that will include a text, readings and assignments that address religious diversity. Two of these readings are Scales, et al. (2002) and Van Hook, Hugen, and Aguilar (2001).

The best example of students struggling to "take seriously the critiques of Christianity offered by proponents of other religions" came on an evening when one of the speakers, an evangelical Christian, received a strong reaction from Jewish members of the audience when he spoke of his understanding of missions. He advocated what he called a "contextual" view of missions — one that acknowledges the many ways in which God reveals Himself, including in religions other than Christianity. This speaker said that a person can come to be a faithful Christ-follower without leaving behind all that she has known and valued in her home culture and her home religion. Hearing this position challenged our students, who worried that he might have compromised too much of Christianity in his efforts to respect other cultures and religions.

What surprised and challenged our students even more, though, came when they saw and heard audience responses to a comment made by this speaker in response to a question. He made it clear that he believes all religions to be expressions of religious longing, a longing that can be fulfilled only in Christ. After this comment, an audible gasp passed through the room. Our students were shocked and confused. They weren't sure whether to feel angry and defensive or guilty and ashamed. In their reflective papers, several made reference to this event and to the sometimes heated table conversations that ensued. This experience helped our students to see how crucial it is to have conversations about religion with those outside of our regular circles of thought and experience. As we discussed in debriefing that evening, had this speaker come to our campus full of Christians, his words would likely have sounded largely reasonable — and even broadminded. Seeing and hearing the pain and anger that his words produced in a more religiously diverse audience was absolutely eye opening for our students!

In identifying outcomes related to what we wanted students to be able to do, we indicated that we wanted them to learn to "use tools of moral conversation." Nash, Bradley, and Chickering describe "moral conversation" as an approach to dialogue that seeks to "open conversational spaces" rather than close them (2008, p.20). For this to occur, they say, all participants need to keep in mind their "core responsibility" which is to "find the truth in what they oppose and the error in what they espouse — before they go on the critical offensive" (p.22). Moral conversation is about "evoking (calling forth), understanding (standing with and among), and affirming (supporting, offering assurance, saying yes instead of no) those defining narratives of meaning that touch all of us" (pp.28-9).

To help students learn these tools, we sought to practice them in class discussions. We talked directly with our students about how important it is to listen carefully and charitably, particularly when it comes to perspectives that we might initially find troubling or challenging. We also sought to frame their written assignments in such a way that it would nudge (or, in some cases, push) students to look for and take time to describe possible connections between their own religious views and practices and those of others. As already noted in some of the student comments above, most were able to find connections across faith lines. In their papers reflecting on the experience of interfaith dialogue as well as through their table discussions in the dialogue sessions, we observed how hard they worked to listen, to ask careful and respectful questions, to affirm what they felt they could affirm. Of course, some were frustrated—both by the reticence that they felt was imposed on them by the emphasis placed on open listening and by the care with which others expressed their own views. One student wrote that he was "alarmed by the reluctance of the speakers and participants to engage in…debate. It seemed as if they were too timid to fully stand for their beliefs." We tried to help students such as this one come to see when debate or a strong presentation of one's views might be productive and when it can be at cross purposes with other important goals (such as making connections with others or learning from them). Particularly for first-year students or others with strongly held views, though, this is a challenge.

Because we teach at a religiously-affiliated university where faculty and students are encouraged to connect their religious beliefs and practices with their academic lives, we are accustomed to talking about spirituality in the classroom. We also are accustomed to helping broaden students' perspectives, particularly through the readings we assign and the questions we ask them. This project has helped us see how much our students' and our own interactions with various ideas are shaped by our campus environment: No matter how hard we might try to imagine ourselves in the shoes of those outside of our own faith traditions, we and our students can't do this very well when we're in a classroom full of Christians who have very similar perspectives. So, first, this project helped impress on us how important it is for us to find ways to help our students engage in interfaith dialogue.

Students are genuinely interested in exploring their own faith and learning about others. Their interactions at the interfaith dialogues demonstrated this, and our having had them participate has encouraged several to want to continue such conversations.

This has helped each of us think more deliberately about various ways in which interfaith issues are important in at least some of the classes we teach—and in our work preparing students for life beyond college. Two of the students in Social and Political Philosophy went on to work with Marion Larson and Sara Shady over the summer of 2008 to further our research on interfaith dialogue. We were awarded research grants from Bethel to complete this research, and both projects have resulted in papers submitted for publication in refereed journals. Using the data collected from our Fall 2008 projects, Marion and a student wrote about the virtues necessary for cultivating healthy interfaith dialogue. Sara and a student explored models of pluralist dialogue to argue for more interfaith dialogue and understanding in the public sphere. The four of us will be presenting on the topic of interfaith dialogue on Christian college campuses at a forthcoming International Forum on Christian Higher Education in Atlanta, Georgia.

Reflecting on the first year of this project, there have been a few challenges in implementation. For instance, it is not yet clear that we've found the best way to engage students in dialogue with religious others. Our students do not yet have good opportunities to interact with peers from other religious traditions, as the overwhelming majority of participants in the interfaith dialogues we've attended are not college-aged. Also the format of the interfaith dialogues does not really allow for the development of long-term relationships that provide the depth students need in order to experience significant change. Each week participants at the dialogues sit at different tables, and facilitation guidelines meant to help encourage carefulness and respect sometimes keep discussions at a surface level. Additionally, the type of person who self-selects to attend and participate in an interfaith dialogue does not necessarily represent the dominant views of any particular religious tradition, so our students at times end up with misconceptions about the faith traditions they encounter.

The second major body of challenges to implementing our projects is logistical. Working at an institution with a heavy teaching load and limited resources further complicates this. Frankly, faculty don't have the time and resources necessary to extend our projects beyond the current level. For example, it is difficult to find and organize enough transportation to take students to and from off-campus events. It is also a big challenge for us and our students to find time to go off-campus on a regular basis for these events. And, although there are several colleges in our area with whom we could network to help facilitate interfaith interaction between students, we do not currently have the time and resources to make these arrangements.

Third our project is limited in scope. From our experience thus far, integrating interfaith dialogue into a course works best when there's a logical connection to a course. Not all of the courses that each of us teaches has a logical interfaith dialogue connection. Looking back, we expected that this project would largely benefit our students, but it's been beneficial for us as well. So many of our interactions are driven by specific purposes or situations that religious topics often don't enter the conversation—except at church when we're surrounded by other Christians. Talking about religious issues across faith lines has been energizing, challenging, and encouraging for us, too. On a personal level we have developed new friendships and collegial relationships. These projects have also fueled several scholarly projects related directly to education as well as other themes. The week we were able to spend at the Institute was invaluable. While there, we learned about activities on other campuses, giving us both encouragement and ideas for our own campus. We received helpful feedback from other participants and from Institute facilitators, enabling us to see both the strengths and potential weaknesses in our initial project ideas. The schedule for the week allowed our team to spend concentrated time working together, in a beautiful setting, away from our home and work responsibilities.

Moving forward, we definitely see ways that we can continue with and expand our project both on our campus and beyond. Within our own community, we would like to help promote conversations with our faculty and student life colleagues to consider ways that we might all do a better job of preparing students to survive and even thrive in a religiously pluralistic world. Perhaps a faculty development initiative could enable us to implement this. Additionally, we'd like to work more deliberately with existing campus initiatives — particularly those in our Reconciliation Studies Program — so that we can partner together and increase capacity.

Beyond our campus we would like to continue being involved with the local interfaith network, building relationships and looking for ways to help connect our students with others their age from varied religious backgrounds. We'd also like to consider partnering with Interfaith Youth Core to promote the development of interfaith relationships through service.

Overall, it's been encouraging to learn that growing numbers of faculty, administrators, and student life staff on a wide range of campuses want to help find ways to prepare students to engage with religion and spirituality. This helps to underscore the importance of projects in religious literacy and interfaith dialogue, and it helps motivate us to keep at it.

Logistically, we've learned to utilize the existing resources at our institution to spark and sustain projects. We encourage other schools to look for support from administrators who are charged with the responsibility to promote respect for diversity. For example, our Chief Diversity Officer is our supporting administrator. We also encourage other institutions to look for funding in unlikely sources. Our initial funding, for example, came from an Alumni Office grant, rather than a faculty development or research grant. This gave us the foundation from which we've been able to apply for further institutional monies and support. Similarly, we've come to see how important it is to build partnerships with various religious leaders and other motivated individuals in our local community. In our case, if the local interfaith network didn't already exist and didn't provide opportunities for interfaith dialogue, it would be much more difficult for us to help students engage in such important activity.

In terms of pedagogy, we've learned that for interfaith dialogue to accomplish much beyond sparking curiosity, there need to be opportunities for longer-term relationships to develop between participants. Our students are learning some basic, yet essential things. For example after one interfaith dialogue event, one of Sara Shady's first-year students remarked, "I never knew people were serious about other religions. I always thought everyone in America was either a serious Christian, a committed atheist, or indifferent about religion." On the other hand, our students need opportunities to grow beyond these initial realizations. They need opportunities in which they'll learn more about the similarities and differences between themselves and others in a way that challenges them to overcome obstacles and learn how to truly engage in meaningful interfaith partnerships beyond college.

References

Eck, D. L.(2003) *Encountering God: A Spiritual Journey from Bozeman to Banaras*. Boston: Beacon, 2003.

Jacobsen, D., & Jacobsen, R.H. eds. (2008) *The American University in a Postsecular Age*. Oxford.

Nash, R.. J., Bradley, D. L. & Chickering, A.W (2008). *How to Talk About Hot Topics on Campus: From Polarization to Moral Conversation*. Jossey-Bass.

Nord, W. A. "Taking Religion Seriously in Public Universities." In Jacobsen and Jacobsen eds. *The American University in a Postsecular Age*. Oxford, 2008. 167-185.

Patel, E. (2007) *Acts of Faith*. Boston: Beacon.

Scales, T. L.,Wolfer, T. A.,Sherwood,D. A. & Garland, D. R. (2002). *Spirituality and Religion in Social Work Practice*. Washington, DC: Council on Social Work Education.

Van Hook, M. P., Hugen, B. & Aguilar, M. (2001) *Spirituality within Religious Traditions in Social Work Practice*. Canada: Brooks Cole..

Appendix A

Fall 2008 Interfaith Dialogue Series

(sponsored by St. Paul Interfaith Network)

My Truth and Your Truth: Absolutes and Openness in Our Religious Traditions
A series of presentations by local religious leaders along with small mixed-group dialogues.

Purpose:

Increase understanding of how our own and other traditions do, or do not, hold "absolutes" regarding religious truth, and "openness" toward others' beliefs and traditions

Provide opportunity for interfaith listening, sharing, constructive dialogue and friendship across religious lines

Discover ways to apply learning from interfaith dialogue

Questions to be addressed will include:

What is your religious tradition's perspective on the beliefs and practices of other traditions?

How do you affirm both absolutes and openness in your religious tradition?

How can our religious traditions support interfaith relationships without sacrificing their uniqueness and authority?

Appendix B

Sample Interfaith Project 1

(from Marion Larson's class)

Several books we're reading together this semester feature characters who are in search of meaning in their lives. Often their journey takes them to (or away from) a particular religious community. Reading about such journeys is an ideal time for us to consider what we have in common with these travelers, where our paths diverge, and what we might learn from them.

This project has two parts—one in which you collect and report on information and one in which you reflect on this information.

Part One: Collecting and Reporting on Information

For each of the options listed below, your research focus should enable you to learn more about a religious tradition that isn't familiar to you—another Christian tradition (such as Pentecostalism, Catholicism, Episcopalianism), another religion (such as Judaism or Islam), or another worship practice (such as fasting or speaking in tongues or confessing sins to a priest).

OPTION ONE: 8 sources

OPTION TWO: Participate in one interfaith dialogue listed below + 5 sources

OPTION THREE: Participate in two interfaith dialogues listed below + 2 sources

Reporting on information collected

Be sure to include sources that are academically credible and appropriate for the topic

Bibliography (MLA format) of sources

For each source, include a summary (around 200 words per source) of information gained from the source

In this portion of your project, you're simply *reporting* on information as clearly and accurately as you can.

Part Two: Reflecting on Information

The primary purpose of this portion of the project is for you to react to and reflect personally on something you learned through the information collection phase of this project. Some questions I'd like you to be sure to address:

At least 300-500 words: How might a believer from your tradition relate to and learn productively from the beliefs and/ or practices of the religious tradition you learned about in this project? (In other words, where is there commonality?)

Around 300-500 words: How did you feel separate from the religious tradition you learned about in this project? You might reflect here on beliefs and/or practices that you learned about. (If you didn't feel separate from the tradition you learned about, then use this portion of your paper to explore questions or concerns that were raised for you through your research and/or through your participation in the interfaith dialogues.)

At least 300 words: What else would you like to say about your experience doing this project?

Appendix C

Sample Interfaith Project 2

(from Sara Shady's class)
PHI323: Social and Political Philosophy
Term Paper
Project Overview

The purpose of this assignment is to explore, analyze, and evaluate an issue related to the topic of religion and contemporary political life. (For example: assess the way in which religion helps or hinders community life, evaluate reasons for or against the use of religion in the public sphere, analyze how religion can influence the formation of civil society, evaluate the role of religion in the American story of peoplehood, or explore the role of religion in forming bonding and bridging groups.) You are expected to demonstrate a solid understanding of relevant course themes and current literature on your topic. Your project may take one of two different forms:

Option 1: Write a paper that integrates your experience of interfaith dialogue with philosophical research. In this option, you must attend and participate in at least 2 of the Saint Paul Interfaith Network dialogues listed on the following page. In your paper you should reflect on how this experience, positively or negatively, influences your thinking about your topic. Your paper must refer to a minimum of *three* contemporary philosophical sources (journal articles or books), of which at least *one* must *not* be an assigned reading from this course.

Option 2: Write a paper based primarily on philosophical research. Your paper must refer to a minimum of *six* contemporary philosophical sources (journal articles or books), of which at least *four* must *not* be assigned readings from this course. You must submit an annotated bibliography of your six sources with your paper.

By Thursday, October 23, you must indicate which option you are going to pursue. You do not need to know your specific topic at this point, however. Feel free to meet with me at any time to discuss the two options or various paper topics!

"Let Everyone Remain Free": The Difficult Dialogues Project at LaGuardia Community College

Robert M. Kahn and Rosemary Talmadge
LaGuardia Community College

The Setting and the Problems To Be Addressed

In many ways, LaGuardia Community College is the prototypical urban community college – founded in 1971 in Western Queens as an open admissions institution, part of the City University of New York, attracting over 15,500 credit students and 35,000 non-credit students, and located in an industrial zone in converted factory buildings. But, in many other ways, LaGuardia is an uncommon place. First, there is the history of eye-popping innovations sustained over long periods of time. Since its founding, LaGuardia has required its students to engage in cooperative education and has played a leading role in the cooperative education movement. LaGuardia was an early pioneer in the development of learning communities, successfully merging credit-bearing academic content and non-credit remediation. More recently, LaGuardia has incorporated the construction of student ePortfolios into the rhythms of academic life and has created a dynamic Center for Teaching and Learning and faculty development programs that have merited a TIAA-CREF Hesburgh Certificate of Excellence in 2004.

Second, LaGuardia is an uncommon place because of the student population that the College serves. The Internationalization Task Force (2004) at the College wrote: "We have the world not only knocking at our door, but already sitting in our classrooms" (p. 96). LaGuardia terms itself "The World's Community College," (Mellow, para. 3) with students born in over 160 countries and speaking more than 110 native languages. LaGuardia's diverse student population includes 38% Hispanic, 23% Asian, 18% Black, 14% White, and 7% Other. Over 60% of our students were born outside the U. S.; indeed, half of our incoming students have lived in the United States for less than five years (LaGuardia Office of Institutional Research and Assessment, 2009). In short, LaGuardia is one of the premier gateways for today's immigrant population.

The diversity of Queens is the daily, vibrant reality that permeates every aspect of campus life at LaGuardia. Given the cultural admixture of the student body and surrounding community, nothing is bland at the College. Everything is passionate. One needs to understand that discussions at LaGuardia are invariably profound and passionate. Dialogues are profound because they are not abstract flights of rhetoric, but grounded in the reality of face-to-face encounters across every imaginable boundary as students move between tradition and the quest to become New Americans. Dialogues at LaGuardia are passionate because so many are engaged in coming to terms with history and politics. Thus, one day, the Christian Club decided to pray for its neighbor, the Gay/Straight Alliance; the Gay/Straight Alliance was indignant. On another day, a Japanese student's comment about the enormity of Hiroshima drew a question about the rape of Nanking from a Chinese student, a reference to the Holocaust from a Jewish student,

and a rejoinder from a Muslim student. In such an environment, one crosses a great rugged expanse of space and time
within a mere ten minutes. The journey is perilous, but essential in advancing the intellectual development of our students.
Such dialogue is poignant, productive, and absolutely rivet-
ing.

There is irony in the fact that a campus which can specify
the ethnicity and linguistic backgrounds of its students and
which exults in its diversity cannot speak to the religious diversity of its student body. We can describe the students who
are enrolled in terms of their gender, ethnicity, place of birth,
income level, place of residence, and high school average, but
we have gathered no information on their religious affiliations
and diversity. As Diana Eck (1993) wrote, "Religion is the un-
spoken 'r-word' in the multicultural discussion." (para. 30) With
the world sitting in LaGuardia's classrooms, a long history of
award-winning innovations, and an excellent faculty and staff,
why has generating dialogue on religious diversity been a problem at LaGuardia? Although the answer is somewhat specu-
lative, two factors appear to be at work. First, religious difference is approached with a degree of caution because of its potential combustibility. As one staff member explained: as a
young man, his mother warned him not to discuss religion and
politics with other people. But, since he had long ago dared to
express his political beliefs and engage in red state/blue state
banter, he felt that he had to avoid even more completely the
divisive subject of religion. Besides, while one could subject
politics and politicians to humorous disparagement, humor and
disparagement were almost always absent from discussions of
religion.

Second, religious difference is not the subject of broad, campus-wide discussion because of the attitude that public institutions, in response to the First Amendment's anti-establishment
clause, should create their own "wall of separation" (Jefferson's
Wall of Separation Letter, para. 2) by maintaining a discreet
silence on the subject of religion. Of course, such self-censor-
ship has a deleterious effect on the concept of academic freedom. More importantly, the failure to discuss religious difference in a serious, sustained manner leaves public institutions

of learning ill-equipped to deal with the gathering storm on the horizon as religious-minded individuals increasingly call on colleges to limit academic freedom and stop promoting evolution, stem cell research, and a woman's right to choose. While one might see New York City's urbanity as a shield against threats to academic freedom, members of the LaGuardia community remember that New York was the scene of Mayor Giuliani censoring artwork (Fairness & Accuracy in Reporting, 1999), the removal of Leonard Jeffries as a CUNY department head (*New York Times*, 1993), and the monitoring of Professor Edward Said and others for their pro-Palestinian sentiments (Cockburn, 2006).

Thus, the campus has recognized that religious diversity was a missing and appropriate topic for a campus-wide and community-wide dialogue at LaGuardia. The great majority of our students – and virtually the entire country – is unaware of Queens' role in colonial history as the progenitor of American religious freedom (Oats, 1999). As stated by Evan Haefeli (2007), the 1645 town charter of Vlissingen (modern day Flushing) in the Dutch colony of New Amsterdam provided for "liberty of conscience" (p. 2). But in 1657 Peter Stuyvesant, the Dutch West India Company's governor of New Amsterdam, prohibited all churches but the Dutch Reformed Church and specifically banned worship by Quakers. On December 27, 1657, thirty citizens of Flushing responded to Stuyvesant - at personal risk - with the "Flushing Remonstrance," a call for religious tolerance to which they signed their names. They wrote:

> You have been pleased to send unto us a certain prohibition or command that we should not receive or entertain any of those people called Quakers because they are supposed to be, by some, seducers of the people. For our part we cannot condemn them…We desire therefore in this case not to judge lest we be judged, neither to condemn lest we be condemned, but rather let every man stand or fall to his own Master…[T]he law of love, peace and liberty [is to be extended] to Jews, Turks and Egyptians, as they are considered sons of Adam…[O]ur desire is not to offend…Independent, Baptist or Quaker…[I]f any of these said persons come in love unto us, we cannot in conscience lay violent hands upon them….[W]e are bound by the law of God and

man to do good unto all men and evil to no man. And this is according to the patent and charter of our Town...(Remonstrance, 1657, para. 6).

In 1662, John Bowne of Flushing defied Stuyvesant's ban and permitted Quaker worship in his home. Bowne was imprisoned and eventually banished "on the first ship wherever it may land" (Oats, para. 2). Remarkably, Bowne made his way from his landing place in Ireland to Amsterdam where he argued his case before leaders of the Dutch West India Company. The Dutch West India Company sent a message to Governor Stuyvesant: "The conscience of men ought to remain free and unshackled. *Let everyone remain free*" (Oats, para. 10). Bowne was able to return to Flushing in 1664. His home still stands, the oldest home in Queens, a registered landmark, and a museum since 1945 when – during the tercentennial of Flushing – Bowne House was dedicated as "a national shrine to religious freedom" (Aita, para. 22). Within the most ethnically diverse county in the nation, Flushing remains an exemplar of religious pluralism.

The Difficult Dialogues Project at LaGuardia

How did LaGuardia first get involved in the Ford Foundation's Difficult Dialogues Project? In April of 2005, the LaGuardia Grants Director was working on campus when President Gail Mellow walked into his office. It should be mentioned that the Grants Director does not get a lot of personal visits from the President. She had in her hand the letter that the Ford Foundation had sent out soliciting proposals for their new Difficult Dialogues Project. The Ford Foundation wanted to foster conversations on campuses and in communities on sensitive topics like religious diversity. The President put the letter on his desk and said, "I want this."

We did not know how competitive the application process would be. More than 675 colleges and universities submitted preliminary proposals, 136 were chosen to submit full proposals, and, ultimately, 26 colleges were selected. LaGuardia was in very good company - with Yale, Emory, Barnard, Queens College, and major state universities like Michigan, Nebraska, North Carolina, and Texas. Only two other community colleges were included: Bunker Hill in Massachusetts and Portland in Oregon (Ford Foundation, 2005). The Grants Director, Bob Kahn, and an Executive Assistant to the President, Rosemary Talmadge, were put in charge of the Difficult Dialogues Project at LaGuardia.

Qualitatively, the objectives for the LaGuardia project included establishing strong relationships with a variety of faith-based community organizations and infusing material on religious diversity into credit and non-credit courses. Quantitatively, the objectives included (a) college faculty and staff representatives visiting a minimum of 50 congregations in order to speak about the credit and non-credit opportunities available at the College and inviting participation in "conversation circles" on religious diversity, and (b) a minimum of 15 faculty members participating in a year-long faculty development seminar on the subject of religious diversity and incorporating new units on religious diversity into courses that they teach.

It should be pointed out at the start that the LaGuardia project achieved its most prominent quantitative objectives: 50 houses of worship received visits from LaGuardia faculty and staff, 15 faculty and staff participated in the pedagogy seminar, 42 faculty and staff were trained to facilitate difficult dialogues, and approximately 350 students, faculty, staff, community members, and State Department visitors participated in conversation circles (about 75 individuals in longer, four-session circles and 275 in mini-circles).

Outreach to Houses of Worship

Bob Kahn was in charge of the process of arranging for 50 congregations to accept visits from LaGuardia faculty and staff. Potential volunteers were invited to a meeting to learn what would be required. Thirty-three members of the faculty and staff attended. Potential volunteers learned about the two basic purposes for the visits: (a) In a borough of more than two million people, not every person knows about the College and the College's role as a community resource. (b) The visitors were to introduce the congregants to the upcoming series of conversation circles and invite participation; it was hoped that conversation circle participants would reflect the diverse denominations that would be visited. Eventually, 22 volunteers (7 faculty and 15 staff) actually spoke at houses of worship and the goal of 50 visits was reached. It should be noted that there was nothing scientific about matching volunteers to the congregations they addressed; it was a matter of availability on a particular date, the distance from the volunteer's home, and a sense of whether a volunteer would be able to excel before a large audience or would be more comfortable with a smaller congregation.

Volunteers were prepared for their visits in a number of ways. They received copies of two handouts that could be shared with congregants who expressed an interest in the College and the Difficult Dialogues project: (a) a Directory of Services listing phone numbers that community members could call to access information about the many services provided by the College (e.g., assistance for immigrants, ESL instruction, recreational opportunities, theater, programs for young children and teens, GED instruction and testing) and (b) a business card listing a number that could be called by those interested in participating in the conversation circles. Volunteers also received a copy of a 5 minute script that could be used in addressing congregations. At a later date, the script was translated into Spanish for those volunteers who would be addressing a Spanish-speaking audience. Finally, volunteers were invited to sit with the congregation during Bob's first visit to a house of worship in order to witness an actual church visit.

Ultimately, the goal of visiting 50 diverse congregations was achieved, with the following faith communities and denominations represented: Baptist, African Methodist Episcopal, Assemblies of God, Orthodox and Reform Judaism, Church of Jesus Christ of Latter-Day Saints, Hindu, Islam, Congregational, Seventh-Day Adventist, Roman Catholic, Lutheran, Greek Orthodox, Reformed, Episcopalian, Universalist Unitarian, United Methodist, Religious Society of Friends, Church of God in Christ, United Church of Christ, and Church of Apostolic Faith.

The Difficult Dialogues Pedagogy Seminar

Under the aegis of the Difficult Dialogues Project and under the leadership of Dean Bret Eynon, the Center for Teaching and Learning planned a year-long pedagogy seminar for the 2006-7 academic year. As is the usual practice, faculty members with appropriate expertise were approached to lead the seminar along with Center staff. To recruit participants, a description of the new seminar was included among the upcoming Center offerings that were circulated to faculty during Spring 2006. Faculty from a wide variety of disciplines applied for inclusion and were selected (i.e., English, Humanities, Cooperative Education, Education and Language Acquisition, Social Science, Natural and Applied Science, and Mathematics, plus one faculty member from The English Language Center in the Division of Adult and Continuing Education).

In the first session of the Difficult Dialogues Pedagogy Seminar, in June 2006, seminar facilitators asked participants to share their feelings about allowing discussions of religion to take place in their classrooms. Almost without exception, faculty expressed wariness and concern. Such discussions often become contentious and passionate, they explained. Tapping into students' core beliefs and areas of strong feeling, such discussions can get out of hand, devolving into heated and irresolvable arguments. Faculty felt that they had no knowledge or training that would prepare them to manage such discussions and make them productive. They felt that they themselves were not knowledgeable about religion, and many had complicated relationships to issues of faith in their own lives. Moreover, they were unsure if discussion of religion was possible and appropriate in a public higher education setting.

While such feelings are not uncommon in higher education, LaGuardia faculty face a particular challenge. The worldwide immigrant diversity of Queens, manifested in LaGuardia classrooms, makes the discussion of religious diversity and freedom essential – at the same time, it also makes such discussion extraordinarily complex. Moreover, the community college curriculum at CUNY allows virtually no room for elective courses that could focus directly on the changing role of religion in American life. While LaGuardia students need to learn to grapple with diversity, LaGuardia faculty struggle to find ways to interject discussions of such issues into a curriculum mandated to focus on basic skills acquisition and vocational preparation.

This was the challenge of the Difficult Dialogues Pedagogy Seminar. The goal was to help faculty consider the ways religious diversity was challenging traditional methods of teaching and develop ways to help students understand and deal with this diversity in their classrooms, their workplaces, and their communities. The seminar pursued this goal through three interwoven strands:

1) Religious Diversity and Society. Helping faculty explore the changing role of religion in American life, including in higher education, and increase their familiarity with the faiths common in the LaGuardia classroom.

2) Religious Diversity and Identity. Helping faculty consider their own attitudes about faith as a way of strengthening their abilities to work with others on these challenging issues.

3) Religious Diversity and the Classroom. Helping faculty consider, develop, and implement classroom experiments that integrate discussions of faith into the curriculum in a mindful and constructive fashion.

This pilot seminar was an exciting, thought-provoking experience for faculty participants and seminar leaders. Fifteen participants completed the seminar and implemented their new curricular experiments, impacting more than 300 students. Faculty feedback, lesson write-ups, and reflections demonstrate that the seminar had a positive effect and laid a solid foundation for extending this work to a broader cohort of LaGuardia faculty and students.

The Difficult Dialogues Pedagogy Seminar took place over 12 months. There were three full days of a summer faculty institute and two full days of a mid-year institute, punctuating a series of 8 half-day seminars, held monthly throughout the academic year. The seminar wove the three strands of discussion outlined above through this extended and demanding meeting structure. Throughout the seminar, participants read and discussed relevant scholarship, with readings ranging from *A New Religious America* by Diana Eck (2001) to sections of *Forms of Intellectual and Ethical Development in the College Years* by William G. Perry, Jr. (1999) and a special issue of *Change Magazine* (2006) focused on "Religion in the Academy." Each session included a section on "Breaking News," featuring articles and current events illustrating the complex and changing role of religion and faith in the contemporary world.

One of the most successful elements of the seminar was our "Encounter" project. Working in pairs, participants did an intensive project studying particular belief perspectives found in Queens, ranging from Sikhs and Buddhists to Jews, Muslims, fundamentalist Christians, and secular humanists. Participants did not simply engage in reading and research. They were also asked to plan and undertake a visit to a church, temple, or place where these beliefs were practiced. During that visit, they were asked to engage in substantial conversation with those they encountered there. Then they were required to prepare and present a report on what they had learned from this project to the seminar as a whole. Participants considered these projects and the related reports as among the most valuable elements of the seminar.

Participants also undertook collaborative research projects on the history of religious freedom in the United States. Working in small groups, each assigned to a particular period in American history, they researched the evolution of religious freedom from the colonial period through the American revolution, the 19th century, and on through the contemporary period. Each group then presented its findings to the group as a whole, leading to generalized knowledge and lively discussion.

At several points throughout the seminar, participants were invited to reflect upon their own relationship to issues of faith, as a way of better understanding the attitudes they brought to the classroom. During the Spring semester, participants took part in a structured self-exploration and sharing process, called the "C-Group" process, adapted from guided discussions of race and culture and designed to help participants share formative experiences and deepen their personal insights in a safe and thoughtful environment.

The unifying focus for the seminar was thinking about the classroom and considering new ways to teach. This multi-faceted discussion evolved steadily over the course of the seminar. In the Fall, several discussions focused on the topic of facilitating difficult dialogues: What pedagogical skills will help to address issues of religion thoughtfully in the classroom? A range of key topics was considered, including: setting the environment (boundaries, safety, ground rules); process issues (scapegoating, managing "struggles"); and "here-and-now" discussion skills (attending to how religious issues relate to course content or theme, handling the emotional discussions that can emerge). Working together, guidelines for effective discussion of controversial topics were created and shared with the College as a whole at a college-wide convocation.

Meanwhile, faculty began developing ideas for new projects that they could integrate into their curriculum. They identified these projects by the end of the Fall semester. During the Winter mid-year institute, they developed, shared, and got feedback on their plans. Then they implemented their projects during the Spring semester. Some projects took a week or two. Others extended for months. Reflection on their experience with classroom implementation took central stage in the seminar during the latter stages of the Spring.

Coordinated by the Center for Teaching and Learning, LaGuardia's faculty development programs are built around a process of collective inquiry and reflective practice. Classrooms are seen as the site for faculty learning, places where faculty can try out new approaches, observe the impact on students, and develop new forms of expertise. Guided by these principles, the Difficult Dialogues Pedagogy Seminar asked every participant to implement a special project related to the seminar. Faculty demonstrated impressive creativity in meeting this challenge. The projects they developed and tested addressed many different facets of the seminar topic: contemporary religious controversies became the subject for oral communication courses and assignments in composition courses, different versions of the Genesis story focused a course on Western Civilization, the scientific challenges to religion became a topic in a physics course.

Conversation Circles

From the start, the LaGuardia project placed at its core the idea that something valuable would be accomplished if diverse groups could be brought together for intimate conversations about their religious upbringing and spiritual journeys. While there are many dialogic groups and institutes that provide models and materials, LaGuardia looked to the Study Circle Resource Center in Connecticut (now named "Everyday Democracy") for its model and inspiration. Rosemary Talmadge, LaGuardia's Executive Assistant for Organizational Development, had earlier in her career coordinated a major community study circle effort on the subject of race in Hartford, Connecticut.

In order to acquaint the campus community with the notion of study circles and launch the project, Nancy Thomas – a Senior Associate at the Study Circle Research Center - was invited to lead an all-day workshop on March 31, 2006. After an introduction to all aspects of Difficult Dialogues at LaGuardia, Nancy placed the project into the context of growing religious diversity and tension and a decline in the secular public square. She illuminated the principles of the deliberative dialogue movements. At various times during the day, the entire group divided into smaller groups and responded to questions, such as (a) "Are Americans knowledgeable about religions? Do they know enough about their own religions, much less the religions of others?" and (b) "What are the primary issues regarding religion and American public life?"

From April until September, the conversation circle organizers worked with Nancy Thomas to draft a facilitators' guide on religion and public life and plan for facilitator training. The ideal was to train enough facilitators so that each circle had two facilitators who varied in terms of religious background, gender, and faculty vs. staff status on campus.

The project contemplated four sessions (2 hours x 4 weeks) for each circle. (See the Appendix for a detailed discussion of the content of the four sessions.) As a result of these sessions, 40 campus volunteers were trained as facilitators. Using the draft guide for facilitators, the training covered an overview of the study circle process and the job description and roles of the facilitator. There was a demonstration on crafting ground rules and facilitation skills, followed by practice mini-circles where volunteers could develop their skills. From Study Circle Resource Center materials – similar to the current guide for training facilitators made available by Everyday Democracy (2008) – facilitators were advised to: be prepared, use open-ended questions, set the right tone, establish clear ground rules, monitor group progress, be comfortable with silence, err on the side of nonintervention, track the time, end sessions gracefully, and be prepared for common facilitator challenges. The common challenges included shy or too talkative participants, discussions losing focus, dealing with factually untrue statements, tension or open conflict.

In the end, LaGuardia ran a total of nine four-session circles on campus and at the Muslim community's Razi School in Woodside, the Church of Jesus Christ of Latter-Day Saints in Elmhurst, and St. Joan of Arc Roman Catholic Church in Jackson Heights. With only one exception, each circle was sufficiently diverse. For example, the group that Bob Kahn co-facilitated included two Mormons, two Roman Catholics, one Eastern Orthodox, one Seventh-Day Adventist, one Unitarian, and one Baha'i.

Since it was not realistic to expect student participation in longer-term sessions given student family and work responsibilities, it was decided that there should be a special effort to attract students to a mini-session. The Southern Poverty Law Center, in partnership with the Study Circle Resource Center, had created an initiative among high school students called "Mix It Up Dialogues" (Mix It Up, n.d.). The idea was to change the self-segregated cafeteria sitting schemes in high schools and engender cross-group conversations. Adapting this idea, LaGuardia designed a "Mix-It-Up Day," an opportunity for LaGuardia students from various backgrounds to participate in conversation circles over pizza. Rosemary Talmadge and Bob Kahn worked closely with personnel in the Office of Student Life to publicize the event. The central idea was to mix up the student clubs; student clubs normally meet individually on Wednesday afternoons. The event attracted more than 40 students who were thoroughly intrigued by the discussions. Ten of the trained facilitators volunteered to run the student mini-circles. It should also be mentioned that, in the aftermath of Mix-It-Up Day, personnel in Student Life reported that a variety of student clubs continued their conversations or sponsored their own dialogues on religious diversity. For example, the Turkish Students Association sponsored an event entitled "The Necessity of Interfaith Dialogue."

Culminating Event

It is part of LaGuardia's culture to celebrate its successes and showcase its achievements. In its original proposal, LaGuardia's Difficult Dialogues Project announced its intention to hold a culminating event that would bring together the disparate elements of the LaGuardia project and acquaint the campus community with the ways in which the College had interacted with local faith communities and had highlighted the religious diversity of students, staff, and Queens.

Twice a year, the instructional staff at the College come together for a day focusing on the educational mission of LaGuardia. With the cooperation of the President and Academic Vice President, the Spring instructional staff meeting was dedicated to the Difficult Dialogues Project. The day began at 2 P.M. in the College's Little Theater. After remarks describing the project by President Gail Mellow, Academic Vice President Peter Katopes, and Bob Kahn, a keynote address was offered by Professor R. Scott Hanson, Visiting Assistant Professor of History at Philadelphia University (now at the State University of New York at Birmingham). Dr. Hanson was chosen as the keynoter by the project's Advisory Committee because of his knowledge of religious diversity in Queens. Dr. Hanson had served as Project Associate in Harvard's Pluralism Project under Dr. Diane Eck. His doctoral dissertation was entitled "City of Gods: Religious Freedom, Immigration, and Pluralism in Flushing, Queens – New York, 1945-2001." In his address, Dr. Hanson offered a detailed overview of how diverse religious communities had been established in Queens and the current status of religious diversity in the Borough.

To illustrate the nature of the conversation circles, Rosemary Talmadge conducted a mini-conversation circle on stage where veterans of the circles discussed their own religious upbringings and journeys, as well as their experiences as circle participants. A second panel discussed the activities and lessons learned by the members of the pedagogical seminar. This far-ranging discussion touched on visits to faith communities by seminar participants, the design of instructional units, the media focus on religious diversity, and techniques for keeping potentially controversial classroom discussions within bounds. The afternoon ended with a reception and dinner for all who wished to stay.

One of the most satisfying aspects of the LaGuardia project was the extent to which campus individuals were inspired by the College's emphasis on religious diversity and responded by incorporating the Difficult Dialogues theme into their activities in ways totally unanticipated by the leaders of the LaGuardia effort. These serendipitous events occurred throughout the year:

- A faculty member in the Humanities Department created a weekly iRadio program on Difficult Dialogues.
- A program officer at the International Visitor Program of the U.S. State Department heard of LaGuardia's efforts and asked if the College would be willing to host groups of international visitors. Consequently, LaGuardia hosted delegations from South Asia, Thailand, Denmark, and the West Bank. Each group received an introduction to the Difficult Dialogues Project and – except for the Danish delegation where time was more limited – participated in a mini-conversation circle that included LaGuardia faculty and staff.
- Periodically, President Mellow sponsors tours for faculty and staff of neighborhoods in Queens. During the project year, a June 1 "Walking and Trolley Tour of Multi-Religious Flushing" was organized by Dr. Lucinda Mosher, a consultant from The Interchurch Center and the author of three books in a series entitled "Faith in the Neighborhood" – *Belonging* (2005), *Praying* (2005), and *Loss* (2007). Dr. Mosher's tour took advantage of Flushing's extraordinary diversity and featured visits to the Muslim Center of New York, the Hindu Temple Society of North America, the China Buddhist Association, the Sikh Center of New York, the Macedonia AME Church, and the Quaker Meeting House.

What Did We Learn?

To measure both the level of satisfaction and type of impact of key activities, LaGuardia's Difficult Dialogues Project employed a number of instruments, most often participant questionnaires and surveys – but, on occasion, more qualitative measures such as transcripts of reflective statements and summaries of focus group comments. As one might expect, there was a great deal of satisfaction and enthusiasm expressed. There were even glimpses of attitudinal change and hard-to-verify promises of behavioral changes to come. But, what LaGuardia really has learned is less verifiable – but no less certain - for those who led and observed the entire process:

1. Like many public colleges and universities, LaGuardia Community College had never initiated formal relationships with leaders of the local faith communities. This lack of personal contacts and long-standing relationships between the College and the faith communities made the task of organizing a series of community study circles particularly challenging. Our task was further compounded in Queens by the sheer number of potential faith communities, the many languages and cultures represented, and the geographic distance between faith communities in our target region. Though the initial learning curve was steep, our process resulted in a much deeper understanding of our community and the students we serve. We hope to build on this learning as we go forward.

2. Higher education institutions contemplating a project like this would do well to plan at the outset for a multi-year effort. Organizers and facilitators felt the project was just "getting traction" when it was time to stop.

3. At the outset, there was an underlying fear that faculty voices espousing secularism and a clear break between church and state might make a concerted effort to derail the Difficult Dialogues Project. While such an argument was raised at an early meeting – drawing the response that it is important pedagogically to understand the diverse backgrounds of LaGuardia's students, including their religious orientations – a spirited attack on the project never materialized. One can speculate on why there was an absence of opposition.

Reasons might include: the focus on academic freedom as a value to be advanced, the support of the College President and other campus leaders, the obvious sincerity of those who signed on early and wanted a sensitive discussion of faith, the prospect of faculty getting valuable information about what to do when controversial topics enter the classroom, the pride in being selected by the Ford Foundation in a prestigious and very selective competition, the quality and thoughtfulness of the initial presentations and emails describing the project.

4. There is a hunger among faculty, staff, students, and local residents for intimate discussions of fundamental beliefs and life experiences. The seminal event in every conversation circle was the opportunity to speak about one's faith journey and to hear the remarkable, very human, and often surprising tales of others struggling with issues of faith and community. There is unmistakably a longing to belong, a search for one's place. For every individual who came to embrace the faith community that was introduced in his or her youth, there seemed to be an individual who had rebelled or slid or experimented and ended up in a new location on the spectrum of belief. The search was always about people: finding a community of people with whom one felt comfortable and accepted. Preachers, music, rituals, friends, or relatives could all make a difference.

5. The principal product of the LaGuardia Project was a group of people confident in the new skills that they had acquired. The members of the pedagogy seminar felt that they were prepared to deal with all manner of controversy in their classrooms. Some have decided that all of their classes should build ground rules at the start of each semester. All were equipped with tools that could transform contentious moments into teachable moments. The conversation circle facilitators similarly felt that they had acquired valuable tools and techniques for tackling controversial issues. Not just religious issues, but any issue could be channeled toward productive discussion and possible resolution using the methods of the Study Circle Resource Center (as previously mentioned, now called Everyday Democracy). Additionally, to

continue the process of acquiring skills in this area, the college was able to send a team of four faculty and staff to the Institute on Religion in Curriculum and Culture of Higher Education.

6. Beyond the practical purpose of introducing the Difficult Dialogues Project to the community, the visits to houses of worship in Queens also were learning experiences for LaGuardia and its volunteers. One learned about the leadership role and styles of the clergy. One learned about the variety of worship communities – from storefronts to megacongregations, from humble and nondescript settings to historic sites and architectural gems. One learned about the wide variations that exist in terms of the role of music, the dress and special fashions that are found, and the physical arrangements for seating clergy, choirs, honored guests, and church elders.

7. The Study Circle Resource Center model gave the LaGuardia project definition and structure. It provided context and texture. Some of the most prized moments came from following the SCRC procedures and adopting its accoutrements: ice breakers, ground rules, the report cards, the exercise with masking tape down the center of the room and participants physically moving (see the Appendix). LaGuardia found the facilitator training guide and the assistance of SCRC's Nancy Thomas invaluable.

8. LaGuardia had simply never reached out to faith leaders in Queens. Many on campus are surprised to see how far the College has come in a year and to see the warmth with which the project has been embraced by the faith community. Fifty congregations have hosted College visitors. It is estimated that the fifty visits put the College's message before 9,000 congregants. Major faith leaders have been on the LaGuardia campus. The relationship with the Queens Federation of Churches (www.queenschurches.org/) has developed to the point where LaGuardia's President was an honoree at the Federation's annual gala. Community members now view the College as a safe space where issues can be discussed and assistance sought. The challenge for the College will be to harness the energy released by entering into these new relationships.

9. In all projects, some results are fleeting and some last. What are the lasting results of the Difficult Dialogues Project at LaGuardia? (1) The skills of facilitation and of approaching problems through conversations are now part of the campus repertoire. These skills will be called upon on other occasions in the future. (2) Ties to the faith community in Queens have been forged and will lead to future collaborations. (3) Faculty have developed pedagogical techniques for bringing controversial issues into the classroom and have developed new instructional units that welcome issues of religion and spirituality into the classroom. These units will be taught for a long time. These pedagogical techniques will serve faculty over a lifetime. (4) The intimate atmosphere and group bonding created at the first meeting of the conversation circles or during student Mix-It-Up Day will not be forgotten. There is no substitute for the straightforward experience of sharing details of one's spiritual journey with members of a group and being entrusted with their stories.

References

Aita, J. (2008). U.S. religious freedom owes debt to colonists' radical document.

Retrieved February 26, 2010 from the U.S. Department of State's Bureau of International Information Programs website:http://www.america.gov/st/diversity-english/2008/July/20080728133100xlrennef0.9696466.html

The Bowne House Historical Society. Retrieved February 26, 2010 from: http://www.bownehouse.org/

Cockburn, A. (2006) . The FBI and Edward Said. *The Nation.* January 12, 2006 Retrieved February 26, 2010 from: http://www.thenation.com/doc/20060130/cockburn

Eck, D.(1993). The challenge of pluralism. *Nieman Report, XLVII* (2). Retrieved date from http://pluralism.org/articles/eck_1993_ challenge_of_pluralism

Eck, D. (2001). *A new religious America.* San Francisco: Harper.

Everyday Democracy (2008). *A Guide for Training Public Dialogue Facilitators.* Available for download at: http://www.everyday-democracy.org//en/HowTo.aspx

Fairness & Accuracy in Reporting (1999). Giuliani's Pro-Censorship Views Need Balance on Sunday shows. October 8, 1999.. Retrieved February 26, 2010, from http://www.fair.org/index.php?page=1768

Ford Foundation (2005). New Ford Foundation Grants to Promote Academic Freedom and Constructive Dialogue on College Campuses. December 12, 2005. Retrieved February 26, 2010 from: http://www.fordfound.org/newsroom/pressreleases/160

Haefeli, E. (2007). The Text of the Flushing Remonstrance. Retrieved February 26, 2010 from the Bowne House Historical Society website: http://www.bownehouse.org/pdf/Evan_Haefeli_Flushing_Remonstrance.pdf

Hart. E. (1657) Remonstrance of the inhabitants of the town of Flushing to Governor Stuyvesant. Retrieved February 26, 2010, from The Religious Freedom Page website: http://religiousfreedom.lib.virginia.edu/sacred/flushing_remonstrance_1657.html

LaGuardia Community College President's Internationalization Task Force (2004). Internationalizing LaGuardia: The next phase. LaGuardia Community College: Long Island City, NY.

Jefferson, T. (1802). Jefferson's Wall of Separation Letter. Retrieved February 26, 2010, from U.S. Constitution Online: http://www.usconstitution.net/jeffwall.html

LaGuardia Office of Institutional Research and Assessment (2009). *Institutional Profile*. Retrieved February 26, 2010, from LaGuardia Community College website: http://www.lagcc.cuny.edu/facts/facts03/PDFs_profile/complete.pdf

Mellow, G.O. (2010) Breaking New Ground. *About LaGuardia*. Retrieved March 12, 2010, from LaGuardia Community College website: http://www.lagcc.cuny.edu/about/

Mix it up. *Teaching Tolerance, A Project of the Southern Poverty Law Center*. Retrieved February 26, 2010 from the Teaching Tolerance website: http://www.tolerance.org/mix-it-up

Mosher, L. (2005). *Faith in the neighborhood: Belonging*. New York: Seabury Books.

Mosher, L. (2005). *Faith in the neighborhood: Praying*. New York: Seabury Books.

Mosher, L. (2007). *Faith in the neighborhood: Loss*. New York: Seabury Books.

New York Times (editorial) (1993). Due process for Leonard Jeffries. Retrieved February 26, 2010, from the *New York Times Opinion* website: http://www.nytimes.com/1993/05/14/opinions/due-process-for-leonard-jeffries.html?pagewanted=1

Oats, D. (1999). About the Flushing Remonstrance. Retrieved February 26, 2010 from: http://www.flushingremonstrance.org/about.html

Perry, Jr., W. G. (1999). *Forms of intellectual and ethical development in the college years*. San Francisco: Jossey-Bass, Inc.

Religion in the Academy. (2006). *Change: The Magazine of Higher Learning*. 38.2. March-April 2006.

Appendix

Agenda for Conversation Circle Sessions

Session #1 was dedicated to establishing the appropriate atmosphere, constructing ground rules for the circles, and sharing personal histories and perspectives. The session began with a 10-minute icebreaker where, pairing participants into concentric circles, individuals were each given 30 seconds to answer questions, such as: (a) "What is the origin of your first or last name, or something special about your name?" (b) "What is one of your favorite hobbies or pastimes?" (c) "Why are you here? What do you hope to get out of this process?"

After the icebreaker, ground rules for all of the sessions were established. Typical ground rules that included: being punctual, listening before speaking, treating each other with respect, speaking for oneself rather than a group to which one belongs, and allowing one person to speak at a time. One particularly useful rule was, if one felt offended, to merely say "ouch" and the group would pause while the offended individual explained why he or she had taken offense.

Finally, each member of the circle was asked to discuss their religious background and journey. People would discuss the way that they had been raised and whether they had stayed with, or ventured away from, their original religious stance. Invariably, participants were intrigued by the stories they heard; it was a moment of true intimacy and human emotion that bound the participants to each other and virtually guaranteed that circle participants would return for the second session.

Session #2 was designed to clarify issues through an interactive activity called "Where Do You Stand?" For this activity, facilitators ran masking tape down the center of their discussion room and labeled one wall "strongly agree" and the other wall "strongly disagree." Participants were invited to move physically as a variety of statements were read to which they could agree, disagree, or straddle the center line. Statements included: "I know a lot about my own faith." "I know a lot about two or more other faiths." "I talk about religion and faith with a high level of comfort." "Most of my close friends share my beliefs or faith perspective." "I am uncomfortable with people who doubt the existence of God." "Morality in society should be based on religion." "Religion is the cause of much hatred and violence in the world."

Session #3 featured two report cards for participants to fill out. First participants gave letter grades (A to F) to the local community based upon a series of statements that were read out. Statements included: "There are no religious tensions in our community." "In our community, students learn about different faith traditions." "In our community, faith-based leaders provide good role-models." "People of all faiths receive the support and services they need." "In our community, people have an equal opportunity to good jobs." In the second step, participants graded the nation. Statements to which they responded included: "Our nation faces no religious tensions." "The interaction between religion and public life is appropriate." "Our national political leaders reflect the religious diversity of the nation." "Religion plays an appropriate role in public policy-making." "Religion plays an appropriate role during elections." "The government respects the First Amendment."

Session #4 focused on action ideas. What could individuals, groups, and government do to address these issues? The circle brainstormed ideas, as well as identified assets that are available to realize the suggested activities.

Development of a Religious Studies Program at Portland State University

Marvin A. Kaiser, Grant Farr,
and Jennifer Schuberth
Portland State University

Background and Context: Understanding the University

Portland State University is Oregon's public urban research institution. Founded after World War II, it sought to bring public higher education to the place bound residents, including the large group of returning veterans, in Oregon's largest metropolitan area. Over the sixty plus years since its inception, the University has grown to Oregon's largest university with 28,000 students in the 2009/10 academic year. While serving this large number of students, it has also emerged as the most ethnically and racially diverse university in Oregon. Consistent with this growth in its domestic diversity, the University has also attracted the largest group of international students among Oregon's public universities. Of particular note, is the diversity of backgrounds of these international students, with the largest number being from the Middle East, followed by those from Japan and China. As the University has grown and developed, it is now internationally recognized for its commitment to engagement with place. Beginning with its mission statement, embodied in the slogan "Let Knowledge Serve the City," which guides its work, PSU has developed an undergraduate curriculum, a research profile and an administrative structure that has at its core a reflective practice that begins with community engagement.

So how does an understanding of religion, religious practice and religious organizations rise to the surface within Portland State University? Simply stated, it has been the subject of a complex relationship. The Portland metropolitan area, as with most areas of the United States, has had a rich religious history. Religious leaders are acknowledged as important figures in the founding and development of the city. Among the numerous significant roles that religious institutions and leaders have played in the city and region several stand out. First, the many private institutions of higher education originally came to the area through the efforts of religious denominations. They have had and continue to have a major impact on the quality of life in the region. Secondly, from its earliest days, but particularly following WWII and into the present, the religious institutions in the African American community have played a very proud and dominant role in religious, civil rights and social justice issues in the state and Portland community. Oregon is also known for its uneasy alliance with selected religious denominations. Among its more notable early 20th century struggles, religion and religious affiliation became embedded in the legislative and legal actions of the state to limit parochial schools as an option for grade and high school education.

Within Portland State University itself, the very diversity of its student population has helped to raise the consciousness of the University around religious affiliation and practice and the place of religious organizations in the lives of students and faculty. By way of example, University has had a long time presence of the Koinania House in the center of the campus which has served as an independent center for religious denominations serving students and faculty. Early on in its history, through its Center for Middle East Studies, PSU became the destination for many Muslim students from the Middle East. More recently, the University has established a Judaic Studies program and now a city wide Hillel. It is significant to note that the development of both Judaic Studies and the Middle East Studies program, including Islamic studies, has proceeded in a very constructive and mutually supportive manner. We believe this is attributable to successive leaders in both programs who have focused on collaboration and partnership.

On the academic side, there has been a significant array of courses, particularly within the humanities, that have focused on religion and religious issues. There has not been, however, an organized course of study that could be identified as "religious studies." How does one account for this given the relatively rich history of religious issues and religious affiliation in Oregon and the mission of the University to be engaged with place? Several issues stand out in attempting to understand and address this question. The first response is that within a young institution, such as PSU, programs tend to develop based on perceived need and the requisite leadership needed to guide a program's implementation. It is evident that the study of religion, as an organized inquiry in its own right, was not seen to be a major concern or responsibility within the University either by students or faculty. Moreover, there was not a campus faculty member(s) champion to both lead the exploration of need, nor to help carry to curricular implementation.

Closely related to this issue, and of considerable importance in institutional politics, there was an identified resistance to "religious studies" among some faculty. The basis of this resistance is at least twofold. The first identifiable issue is located within the very culture of the state and region. While Oregon has a very active religious institutional history, as noted earlier, and contemporary religious institutional presence, it is also acknowledged as ranking among the highest "unchurched" states in the country. While one might conclude that this ranking is worthy of academic study in itself, it appears to lend itself to a negative attitude about religious studies and negative perceived need of such an academic program on the campus. Related to this issue, is the concern expressed by some that such an academic program is associated with religious proselytizing. While this concern represents a failure to differentiate between intellectual understanding and active religious recruitment, it nevertheless is voiced as a concern in an environment that has a skeptical view of religion and religious affiliation. A third issue focused on academic leadership, that is, the availability of a faculty member(s) within the institution with an academic background in religious studies. In lieu of such disciplinary leadership, efforts to develop the program relied on faculty with related program interests from other disciplines and on local clergy to support and teach courses supportive of religious studies. This approach proved to be unsustainable. Finally, in a long standing environment of scarce fiscal resources, any new academic program without its own dedicated internal or external resources is under special scrutiny to provide a rationale for its implementation in a manner that will not draw resources away from existing programs.

Religious Studies at Portland State University

It is within this background and context that Portland State University has recently sought to develop a formal religious studies program. As a large, urban public university with an access and engagement mission, several faculty and administrative leaders believe it is important to help students develop an understanding of, and literacy about, religion and religious practice as a significant part of their academic work at the university. It was also understood that for many students who may perceive the urban university environment as alien to their religious experience, a religious studies program would provide them with opportunities to contextualize their own religious traditions and to honor these traditions as worthy of serious academic study.

Given this background it was important that a convergence of events provided the grounding for the program to develop. The key ingredients to this convergence are related to the programmatic leadership of the Society for Values in Higher Education (SVHE). The first of these seminal events occurred with the convening of the Wingspread Conference on Religion and Public Life by the SVHE in the summer of 2007. That conference and its subsequent Wingspread Declaration identified the key importance of religious literary, religion and academic discourse and students' search of spirituality. Participation in that conference reaffirmed the need and commitment of the PSU participant to reinvigorate the discussion on the PSU campus to address the possibility of an organized religious studies program. Fortuitously, SVHE followed the Wingspread Conference with a Jessie Ball duPont supported project to invite interested higher education campuses to participate in a process to explore and develop a religious study's program appropriate for their campus. (This project is described in earlier chapters.) PSU convened a group of faculty and administrators to determine both their interest and commitment to such a process. The positive response of the group was such that PSU became an institutional partner in the project.

Three members of the project team participated in the SVHE Institute on Religion in Curriculum and Culture of Higher Education at the Trinity Conference Center in the summer of 2008. The conference was a catalyst for the team, providing time and mentoring for the religious studies proposal to mature. As a result of this process, the team, with the assistance of the conference faculty, developed a curricular plan for a Religious Studies minor at Portland State University that included a statement of need, a curricular design and implementation strategy and a business plan to match. It is noteworthy that this original plan developed at the conference focused on religious studies within the urban context.

Upon returning to PSU, the team brought the refined curriculum proposal for a minor in religious studies within the College of Liberal Arts and Sciences to the larger team. To focus its work, the team proposed a program that would have religious literacy as its central focus, with a clearly defined set of learning outcomes for students. To this end, all students in the program would be able to:

1) Describe and compare the major features of the major world religions and their traditions;

2) Analyze the relationship between a religious tradition and a culture to which it belongs, explaining how it shapes and is shaped by surrounding society;
3) Delineate how scholars have defined "religion," evaluate the strengths and weaknesses of those definitions, and discuss the methodologies arising from various definitions.
4) Use scholarly terminology in describing and analyzing religions;
5) Interact and communicate with people from different religious traditions in a competent and sensitive manner.

Leadership

At that point in our process, the second necessary ingredient occurred – the emergence of a faculty member, new to the campus, with a strong academic background in religious studies, with both the ability and the interest to provide leadership to the program. This faculty member had been serving at the University in another instructional capacity, unrelated to the religious studies program. This individual was asked to serve as the coordinator of the program and led the development of a formal curriculum proposal during the fall term, 2009. In the meantime, the new Coordinator of Religious Studies is teaching two required introductory courses for the minor (Introduction to World Religions and Introduction to the Study of Religion) as Humanities courses. The Coordinator is also laying the groundwork for the program—developing the website (http://www.pdx.edu/religiousstudies/), building a base of interested students, organizing public programming, working on fundraising and development and organizing a faculty steering committee.

Curriculum Plan

This project (the development of a minor in Religious Studies) targets undergraduate students at PSU. Given its large number of transfer students, it also includes articulation agreements with two-year colleges in the Portland metropolitan region to enhance the program's accessibility for their students.

As a first step in the PSU curricular approval process, the

College of Liberal Arts and Sciences Curriculum Committee received and approved the program proposal in December, 2009. The program was submitted to the University Curriculum Committee and the Faculty Senate for full approval in Spring, 2010 (see Appendix).

The curriculum plan includes an assessment plan to determine how effectively the learning outcomes have been achieved. To this end, the Religious Studies minor will implement a five-year assessment plan to evaluate the effectiveness of the program in achieving its student learning outcomes. This plan will include indirect measures, such as student surveys and syllabus analysis, as well as direct measures of student work, including rubric-based evaluation of student writing samples, presentations, and/or course portfolios. The results of these assessment activities will inform course content and curriculum development.

Student assessments have been collected from the initial course "Introduction to World Religions." Students were asked about their perspectives on the course, as well as suggestions for improvement. Respondents indicated that they learned about religious traditions other than their own and gained a better understanding of what animates religious beliefs and practices. These assessments also indicated that students desire additional religious studies courses.

Successes of the Project

The successes of the program are as follows:
a. The development of a complete program proposal which is moving through the University approval process;
b. Course proposals and complete syllabi for the three core courses in the Religious Studies minor;
c. Curriculum and course approval from the College of Liberal Arts and Sciences Curriculum Committee;
d. The appointment of a new faculty member with a Ph.D. in Philosophy of Religion from the University of Chicago to teach and advise students interested in Religious Studies and to lead the development of the Religious Studies program as it moves from being a proposal to an approved program;

e. The first course, "Introduction to World Religions," was offered in the fall term, 2009, under a general humanities course code with a full enrollment of 58 students;

f. The "Introduction to World Religions," offered again in the winter term, 2010, was filled to capacity within the first week of early registration;

g. A large number of faculty from across the campus and from regional higher education institutions have expressed interested in contributing to the religious studies program through lectures and in building public programming.

Challenges

The development and implementation of the religious studies minor at Portland State University, has encountered a set of challenges.

The first challenge centered around the uncertainty by selected members of the academic community about the necessity and desirability of such a program. This challenge appeared to be based on two concerns. The first was focused on the concerns about the academic standing of religious studies. The second focused on concerns about the role such a program might play in fostering religion and religious practices. The program has been able to progress as both of these concerns were, and continue to be, addressed by the leadership of the program.

The second challenge was to find appropriate leadership for the program. While several faculty and administrators have given support to the development of a religious studies program, the program lacked the leadership of a faculty member with specific religious studies academic background. During 2009 an individual was employed by the University in another instructional capacity who had the academic background and desire to help lead a religious studies program. By being able to bring this individual into the program it gave the religious studies both focused leadership and academic credibility.

The third challenge to implementation of a religious studies program at PSU has been the institutional budget uncertainties over several years and especially during the economic downturn over the past two years. As the academic planning for the program continued, the College of Liberal Arts and Sciences and the University was able to find the resources in Summer, 2009, to dedicate a faculty line for program leadership and instruction. This fiscal decision was the final and key piece of the strategy that allowed the plans for the implementation of the religious studies program to succeed.

Benefits

The challenges have been offset by a number of benefits that have arisen from our process. The first is that it allowed the University to bring together faculty members with an interest in religious studies from around the campus. Faculty from the following departments are either offering classes with religious studies content and/or would like to develop courses with more religious studies content in the future: Art History, Anthropology, English, History, Judaic Studies, Philosophy, Sociology, and Women's Studies. In this way, PSU has been able to create a community of faculty that may not otherwise have seen connections between their work. Second, the program allows the University to address a vital student need that has become only more apparent. In student assessments of the Introduction to World Religions, the majority of students said they would like to take more religious studies courses and a number indicated that they would like to minor or major in religious studies. The coordinator has also been approached personally by a number of students inquiring about future classes and has received numerous emails from current and prospective students interested in the minor.

Lessons Learned

The major lesson learned comes not only from the development of the religious studies program, but from a several year process of attempting to develop a program that had more failures than successes. The lesson learned is that religious studies can be a controversial and therefore difficult program to start. "Religious studies" means different things to different people, and can bring with it great emotion and passion, both for and against it. When a school starts a religious studies program, especially at a public institution, it must be aware of the potential pitfalls that may arise. The individual(s) developing and implementing such a program must be able to speak to these concerns, including the ability to articulate to faculty and administrators the academic legitimacy and value of religious studies while maneuvering the fiscal strategies necessary to ensure the program's long term viability.

Future Plans

As noted above, once the Religious Studies program has been officially approved and the minor has been established, the University will consider the development of a Religious Studies major. In keeping with the PSU mission of engaging with its community and region, the program is also in the process of developing a series of public programs that will expand religious literacy beyond the boundaries of the campus. This effort will include a regular program of public lectures by leading religious studies scholars, as well as collaboration with other educational institutions, including neighboring colleges and universities, and not for profit agencies such as the local Council on Humanities, World Affairs Council and Literary Arts.

Appendix

Proposal for a New Academic Program (Excerpted)

Institution: Portland State University
College/School: College of Liberal Arts and Sciences
Department/Program: Religious Studies Minor

1. Program Description

a. Brief overview (1-2 paragraphs) of the proposed program, including its disciplinary foundations and connections; program objectives; programmatic focus; degree, certificate, minor, and concentrations offered.

The Religious Studies Minor will be an academic interdisciplinary program within the College of Liberal Arts and Sciences. Its intellectual mission will be to introduce students to the academic study of religion and expose them to a variety of religious traditions. Specifically the program will investigate the relationship between religious beliefs and practices and the formation of culture, conceptions of human identity, and moral and ethical frameworks. It will offer students the opportunity to investigate academically the diverse meanings of religious practices in human experience from various disciplinary perspectives including those of history, sociology, anthropology, philosophy, literature, women's studies, ethnic studies, international studies, and the arts. The objectives of the Religious Studies program are to broaden and deepen students' knowledge of religious traditions around the world, to foster an awareness of how religious discourses and practices affect the lives of individuals and societies, and to provide an opportunity for students to engage with diverse religious communities in the Portland metropolitan area. Initially, the program will offer a minor, with the expectation that a major will be offered in the future.

b. Course of study – proposed curriculum, including course numbers, titles, and credit hours.

The minor in Religious Studies is designed to fit the particular interests of each student, who will choose a set of electives in consultation with the Program Advisor.

To earn a minor in Religious Studies, a student must complete 28 credit hours of approved course work, including the following:

Foundational courses (12 credits):
- RSt 201 Introduction to Religious Studies I (4)
- RSt 301 Introduction to Religious Studies II (4)
- RSt 415 Contemporary Issues in Religion (4)

Elective courses (with advisor approval) (16 credits):
- At least two courses from the same religious tradition. Traditions are dependent on current offerings and may include the following: Judaism, Christianity, Islam, Hinduism, Buddhism, Taoism, Confucianism, Native American Religions, Caribbean Religions, African Religions. (Some courses may address more than one tradition. Advisor approval will be based on class syllabi.)
- At least two courses in the same area. Areas include: (1) Religion and the Human Sciences; (2) Religion and the Humanities; (3) Historical Studies in Religion.

The following courses have been approved based on review of syllabi and/or discussions with faculty. These classes include omnibus courses that include "Special Topics" courses (399 and 410/510) and seminars (407/507) which may be appropriate, depending on the focus of the particular offering. Advisor approval will be based on course syllabi.

Religion and the Human Sciences:
- ANTH 317 Peoples and Cultures of South Asia (4)
- ANTH 430/530 Myth, Ritual and Symbol (4)
- ANTH 432 Gender in Cross Cultural Perspective (4)
- ANTH 430/530 Symbolic Anthropology Discussion (1)
- ANTH 447 Advanced Topics in South Asian Anthropology (4)
- SOC 410/510 Family and Identity through Film (4)

Religion and the Humanities:
- ARH 311 History of Asian Art I (4)

- ARH 312 History of Asian Art II (4)
- ARH 313 History of Asian Art III (4)
- ARH 411 Chinese Buddhist Art (4)
- ARH 412 Japanese Buddhist Art (4)
- ARH 407/507 Religion and American Art (4)
- ENG 308 Jewish Literature: Messiahs in Modern Jewish Literature (4)
- ENG 318 The Bible as Literature (4)
- ENG 330 Jewish and Israeli Literature (4)
- ENG 410 Cities of Modern Jewish Literature: Baghdad (4)
- ENG 410 Writing the Holy Land (4)
- ENG 410 Sages and Mystics: Post-biblical Jewish Literature (4)
- PHL 210 Philosophy of Religion (4)
- PHL 319 Introduction to Asian Philosophy (4)
- PHL 315 Existentialism (4)
- PHL 399 Medieval Philosophy (4)
- PHL 302 History of Philosophy (4)
- PHL 416/516 The Rationalists: Descartes, Leibniz, Spinoza (4)
- PHL 417/517 The Empiricists (4)
- PHL 421 19th Century Philosophy (4)
- PHL 451 Classical Figures (when appropriate)(4)
- WS 410 Women Mystics (4)
- WS 410 Feminist Biblical Interpretation (4)

Historical Studies in Religion:
- HST 199/399 Introduction to Judaism (4)
- HST 314 History of the Ancient Near East (4)
- HST 320 East Asian Civilizations (4)
- HST 350 English History from 1066 to 1660 (4)
- HST 399 Modern Jewish History: From the Enlightenment to Crisis (4)
- HST 399 The Holocaust (4)
- HST 424/524 Topics in Chinese Though and Religions: Confucianism (4)
- HST 454/554 Topics in Medieval History: The Holy Land Before the Crusades (4)

- HST 454/554 Topics in Medieval History: The Holy Land in the Crusader Era (4)
- HST 454/554 Topics in Medieval History: History of Christianity to 1500 (4)
- HST 454/554 Topics in Medieval History: The Holy and the Damned: Sanctity and Deviance in the European Middle Ages (4)
- HST 454 Jewish Life & Culture in the Middle Ages (4)
- HST 461 Topics in Jewish History: Eastern European Jewish Society & Culture (4)
- HST 495/595 Comparative World History: Islam and Modernity (4)
- INTL 317 Japanese Religious Traditions (4)
- INTL 410 Topics: Islamic Movements (4)
- INTL 201 Introduction to Islam (4)

Total: 28 Credits

Other courses may be developed and introduced during the first five years of the Program's existence. Based on the courses offered through similar programs at comparable institutions, courses addressing the following topics may be included:
- The historical development of a particular religious tradition or movement
- Beliefs and practices of a specific religious tradition or movement
- Interactions between specific religious traditions or movements
- Relation between marginalized groups and a specific religious tradition or movement
- Gender and a specific religious tradition or movement
- Religion and sexuality
- Mysticism
- Religion in the urban setting
- Religions of a particular region or nation (e.g. Pacific Northwest, Asia, United States)
- Atheism, agnosticism, secularism, and doubt

- New religious movements (the origins, development, and growth of religious movements founded in the 19th and 20th centuries)
- Religious fundamentalism
- Reading and conference courses on religious topics, conducted either with Religious Studies faculty or with faculty from other departments with Program Advisor approval.

c. Manner in which the program will be delivered, including program location (if offered outside of the main campus), course scheduling, and the use of technology (for both on-campus and off-campus delivery).

The Minor in Religious Studies will be located at the main PSU campus. RSt 201, RSt 301, and RSt 415 will be offered as a yearly sequence beginning in fall term. It is anticipated that each required course will be offered once each year, however should student interest indicate greater demand, the RSt 201 and RSt 202 may be offered more than once each year. The required courses will also be offered in the evenings.

d. Ways in which the program will seek to assure quality, access, and diversity.

Systematic program-level assessment to evaluate and improve the Religious Studies minor will begin from the Program's inception. Quality will be assured through a three-year assessment plan to measure the degree to which the program's student learning outcomes are being met by the current curriculum and course designs. This plan will include indirect measures, such as student surveys and syllabus analysis, as well as direct measures, including the rubric-based evaluation of student writing samples, presentations, and/or course portfolios. Assessment results will be used to improve the structure and content of individual courses, and will also inform curricular design and revisions to student learning outcomes as the program grows.

Religious tradition and faith identification are important dimensions of diversity. The Religious Studies Minor will strive to bring students from diverse ethnic and cultural backgrounds into the minor to broaden the range of perspectives present in the classroom. The Program will offer students from a variety of religious traditions the opportunity to contextualize their own traditions through the academic study of religion, while also enabling students without strong religious affiliations to analyze the complexities of religious experience. To bring a diverse cross-section of students into Religious Studies, the Program will reach out to culture- and faith -based student groups on campus, as well as to students already enrolled in courses that qualify as electives for the minor, and in Freshman and Sophomore Inquiry courses on related themes.

Furthermore, an important component of the Religious Studies minor will involve direct contact with religious communities in the Portland metropolitan area, primarily through RSt 415. Students will learn about oral history and conduct their own interviews with members of religious organizations around themes such as religion and migration. By building relationships with these communities through contact with students in RSt 415, the Religious Studies minor will also increase contact with and access to the university among some groups that have historically been underrepresented in higher education.

e. Anticipated fall term headcount and FTE enrollment over each of the next five years.

We anticipate that the program will generate considerable student interest even in the first years. Introduction to World Religions, which was offered this past fall under HUM299 and will be RSt 201, enrolled fifty-eight students and this term has fifty students and had a waitlist of 10. We had to lower the cut-off because of room availability. Therefore, we predict that we will enroll approximately 400-500 students in the first five years producing 1600 student credit hours.

f. Expected degrees/certificates produced over the next five years.

It will take at least two years before minors can be awarded. Approximately 5 to 10 degrees will be awarded after the second year. Therefore we expect to give between 20 and 30 degrees in the next five years.

g. Characteristics of students to be served (resident/nonresident/international; traditional/nontraditional; full-time/part-time; etc.)

The Religious Studies minor will be available to all interested undergraduate students at PSU. Through its diversity recruitment efforts, the program hopes to involve many nontraditional students, and may be particularly attractive to students from strong faith traditions, many of whom come from groups that have historically been underrepresented in higher education. Through courses offered at a variety of times and days and in hybrid and/or online formats, participation in the Religion Studies minor will be accessible for part-time students as well as full-time students, and for students balancing work and family obligations with their studies.

h. Faculty resources

Most of the program can be offered with the current faculty. A 1.0 FTE faculty member will be added the first year of the program. Currently, the .5 FTE Instructional Faculty. position is held by Dr. Jennifer Schuberth, Ph.D. in Religious Studies from the University of Chicago. The program will use the facilities of the Office of the Dean of CLAS for clerical and office support.

i. Facilities, library, and other resources.

The PSU Library's resources can support the Religious Studies Program's basic needs at this time. Beyond office space and supplies for new faculty attached to the program, no special facilities or equipment are needed.

j. Anticipated start date.

As soon as program receives approval.

2. Relationship to Mission and Goals

a. Manner in which the proposed program supports the institution's mission and goals for access; student learning; research, and/or scholarly work; and service.

The Religious Studies Minor will support Portland State University's mission of access by making the academic study of religion available at a range of times in both classroom and online instructional formats. As an interdisciplinary field,

Religious Studies is uniquely suited to address Portland State University's Blueprint for the Future.

The Religious Studies Program will Provide Civic Leadership Through Partnership by presenting opportunities for both students and faculty to develop relationships with the community through course work and public programming. Speakers and events sponsored by the Program will serve interested groups and individuals from the entire metro area, and community engagement through RSt 415 will be a key part of the curriculum for students completing the minor. Through public programming and civic engagement, the Religious Studies program will Expand Resources and Improve Effectiveness by establishing a reputation within the Portland Community as a source for intelligent debate about religion. This public profile will lead to both greater awareness of the programs offered at PSU, and to donor interest in the Program and the University.

The presence of the Religious Studies Program at Portland State University will Improve Student Access by demonstrating to prospective students of various religious traditions that the University recognizes the importance of religion in the human experience, and considers religious traditions to be a worthy area of academic inquiry. Through articulation with the burgeoning Religious Studies course offerings at Portland Community College, this program will also support the transfer process for community college students, thus Enhancing Educational Opportunities in the region.

The Religious Studies Program will Achieve Global Excellence by distinguishing the university in an area of research it currently lacks. The Program will also better prepare students to participate in a global economy by helping them understanding the interplay between religion and social and economic practices.

b. Connection of the proposed program to the institution's strategic priorities and signature areas of focus.

The Religious Studies curriculum is designed with Portland State University's strategic priorities and signature areas of focus at its heart. Religion is an important dimension of human diversity, and the academic study of world religious traditions will help students contextualize their own religious and/or secular upbringing within the broad range of human experience. The Program will enhance educational opportunities and improve student success by helping students learn to communicate effectively with individuals from other religious traditions, and to recognize how personal beliefs and practices affect various forms of community and scholarly engagement. The Program will provide civic leadership through partnerships through public programming and community contact in RSt 415, which may include interviews with members of local religious organizations and visits to local religious communities and organizations. Public programming will also expand resources by making PSU's programs visible to prospective students and donors. Religious Studies will also help achieve global excellence by helping students explore the evolving relationship between religion and the processes of globalization.

c. Manner in which the proposed program contributes to Oregon University System goals for access; quality learning; knowledge creation and innovation; and economic and cultural support of Oregon and its communities.

The Religious Studies Minor's contributions to OUS and Portland State University's shared goals for access and quality learning are addressed in 2 (a) and (b), above. In addition to filling a scholarly gap at PSU by hiring faculty engaged in knowledge creation in the field of Religious Studies, the Program will have an innovative local focus, emphasizing the role that religious groups play in Portland's community life (primarily through RSt 415). As a community-oriented program, Religious Studies will both create knowledge regarding this aspect of culture in Portland and Oregon, and host speakers and events that support and serve cultural interests in the region.

Religious communities and faith-based organizations play a significant role in the urban and regional economies, and students who are familiar with the religious diversity of the region and able to communicate effectively with people from religious traditions other than their own are better equipped to succeed professionally, and to improve services in many fields, including education, public and non-profit administration, social services, health care, human resources, and other sectors that deal with diverse populations. Furthermore, students who understand the variety of human religious experience are also better prepared to function effectively in a globalizing economy and the increasingly complex field of international relations, in which religious identities and ideologies play a central role.

d. Manner in which the program meets broad statewide needs and enhances the state's capacity to respond effectively to social, economic, and environmental challenges and opportunities.

As the Portland metropolitan area grows rapidly, it is becoming increasingly diverse and a greater range of religious traditions are present in its communities than ever before. For students at PSU, most of whom remain in the state after graduating, learning to understand this diversity and communicate with individuals from a variety of religious traditions will enhance their ability to succeed in their workplaces and provide quality service to these groups in both the public and private sectors. This could be particularly beneficial to students going into fields involving community outreach (including sustainability activism) or the provision of services such as education, healthcare, and social work. The ability of these graduates to work successfully with Portland's religiously diverse population will benefit the entire community.

Additionally, students with an understanding of religious diversity will be better positioned to operate successfully in a globalizing economy. By fostering these qualities among students likely to stay in Oregon, the Religious Studies Program will be contributing to the state's economic potential on a global playing field.

3. Need
a. Evidence of market demand.

Introduction to World Religions (HUM299) was offered this fall and saw full enrollment at 58 students. The class is being offered again this winter and has full enrollment at 50 (room limitations led to lower class size). In class assessments, students in the Introduction to World Religions course indicated they wanted to take more religious studies courses and many inquired about the minor. Since September, when the Religious Studies program had a website, the advisor has received numerous emails from current and prospective students asking about the religious studies minor. Further evidence for this demand can be found at Portland Community College, where recent experimental courses in World Religions filled quickly, and students who completed those classes clamored for additional course offerings in the subject.

b. Manner in which the program would serve the need for improved educational attainment in the region and state.

By providing a program in which religion is both taken seriously and critically examined, the Religious Studies Minor will offer students who identify as religious the opportunity to think academically about a topic of central importance in their lives. At the same time, it will provide all participating students, whether religious or not, with an understanding of the diversity of religious experience. This will help make our large urban university a more open and hospitable learning environment for students from a range of religious traditions, which supports current retention and graduation initiatives. Furthermore, as the Religious Studies Minor builds and sustains relationships with religious communities throughout the Portland metropolitan area, these points of contact could potentially improve access to higher education for members of those communities, as well.

c. Manner in which the program would address the civic and cultural demands of citizenship.

In a globalizing economy and an increasingly diverse region, an understanding of religious diversity has emerged as an important aspect of intercultural communication and civic engagement. With its emphasis on community engagement, the Religious Studies Program complements the academic and professional path of any student-citizen. Additionally, by hosting speakers and other public events, the

Religious Studies Program will create many opportunities for members of the wider Portland community to gather and engage issues of religion.

4. Outcomes and Quality Assessment
a. Expected learning outcomes of the program.
> Successful PSU Religious Studies minors will be able to:
> 1) Describe world religious traditions and compare their key features.
> 2) Analyze the relationship between a religious tradition and a culture to which it belongs, explaining how it shapes and is shaped by surrounding society.
> 3) Delineate how scholars have variously defined "religion," evaluate the strengths and weaknesses of those definitions, and discuss the methodologies arising from various definitions.
> 4) Use scholarly terminology in describing and analyzing religions.
> 5) Interact and communicate with people from different religious traditions in a competent and sensitive manner.

b. Methods by which the learning outcomes will be assessed and used to improve curriculum and instruction.
> The Religious Studies minor will implement a three-year assessment plan to evaluate the effectiveness of the program in achieving its student learning outcomes. This plan will include indirect measures, such as student surveys and syllabus analysis, as well as direct measures of student work, including rubric-based evaluation of student writing samples, presentations, and course portfolios. The results of these assessment activities will inform course content and curriculum development.

c. Program performance indicators, including prospects for success of program graduates (employment or graduate school) and consideration of licensure, if appropriate.
> The initial program performance indicator for the Religious Studies minor will be the number of students who successfully complete the minor, particularly as a percentage of the number who enter the Program. As the Program grows

and is able to offer a major, performance measures will include determining the success of graduate majors in terms of employment or acceptance to and completion of graduate programs.

d. Nature and level of research and/or scholarly work expected of program faculty; indicators of success in those areas.

The initial faculty in Religious Studies will be expected to produce research and scholarly work appropriate to the level and rank of their position consistent with the standards in other CLAS academic programs and departments. Specifically, the faculty members in the program will be expected to develop a consistent and substantial publication record in peer reviewed journals in the appropriate intellectual areas or the publications of monographs and to be active in seeking external funding to support the program as well as their own research.

5. Program Integration and Collaboration

Ways in which the program complements other similar programs in other Oregon institutions and other related programs at this institution. Potential for collaboration.

The proposed PSU Religious Studies Minor complements other programs in the state by focusing on the role of religious institutions in Portland. This focus takes recognition of the important role religious thought and practice have played and continue to play in the lives of groups and individuals — including students — while using the rich religious diversity of the local environment as a unique learning opportunity. Because several private colleges and universities in the Portland metropolitan area also offer majors and/or minors in Religion or Religious Studies, there is great potential for collaborating on events, workshops, and service-learning opportunities. As noted, there is also potential for forming a Religious Studies articulation agreement with Portland Community College.

The Religious Studies Program also complements the existing Judaic Studies program at PSU, and will collaborate with that growing program through joint course offerings and co-sponsorship of public workshops and lectures.

6. External Review

The Religious Studies Program will engage in a regular and systematic external review process in accordance with the schedule maintained by the College of Liberal Arts and Sciences.

PART THREE –
Moving Forward

Religious Literacy and Public Schools

Robert A. Spivey
Florida State University

Every day, in depressing array, we are bombarded with evidence of our nation's appalling religious illiteracy. Hordes of American citizens perceive Islam, the religion of 1.6 billion people, as a purveyor of terrorism; neighbors raise concerns regarding the building of a nearby Morman house of worship, and a widely known commentator has stated that churches that are concerned with social justice issues are not truly Christian institutions.

In American society citizens suffer from an inadequate understanding of religion, largely because most have never studied their own religion or that of others. This is due to such mixed motives as timidity, misconception, religious zeal, and indifference. Those who do engage in study about religion do so generally late in their formal schooling, at the college level, where religion study is sometimes fascinating and sometimes offensive. Is it surprising then that we have large numbers of citizens who view religion simplistically and even larger numbers for whom religion is a matter of convenience or indifference?

This neglect of learning about/from religion extends beyond elementary and secondary schools to the higher education level – most recently and cogently depicted in Stephen Prothero's *Religious Literacy: What Every American Needs to*

Know – and Doesn't (2007), a *New York Times* non-fiction bestseller. A comment on the back cover of this book states:

> At a time when many regard religion as the problem tearing America's societal fabric, *Religious Literacy* argues that religion can be the solution if Americans regard the commonalities of principles and values underlying their faith traditions as the thread that sews it back together (Imam Feisal Abdul Rauf, 2007).

And Prothero introduces his thesis with the following story:

> A few years ago I was standing around the photocopier in Boston University's Department of Religion when a visiting professor from Austria offered a passing observation about American undergraduates. They are very religious, he told me, but they know next to nothing about religion. Thanks to compulsory religious education (which in Austria begins in elementary schools), European students can name the twelve apostles and the Seven Deadly Sins, but they wouldn't be caught dead going to church or synagogue themselves. American students are just the opposite. Here faith without understanding is the standard; here religious ignorance is bliss....One of the most religious countries on earth is also a nation of religious illiterates (p. 7).

Before Prothero and this current generation, we were in worse shape as to religious literacy because until the mid-1960s there was virtually no religion-study in the academy, except in private colleges and seminaries. The 1962 and 1963 Supreme Court declared that public education should avoid the practice of religion. In these same opinions, the court declared that the proper role of public schools included study *about* religion. As a result, the decade of 1965-1975 witnessed an explosion of religion departments at public universities such as the University of Virginia, Indiana University, Penn State, Florida State University, University of North Carolina-Chapel Hill, University California at Santa Barbara, University of Tennessee, University of Montana.

During this period there were also several major phoenix-like efforts to extend religion-study into the public schools. At Indiana University there was a partially successful effort led by Thayer Warshaw and Jim Ackermann to initiate in Indiana schools courses in *The Bible as Literature* with curricular and teacher education components that were both legally and educationally sound. At Penn State University, a public high school senior level course and textbook were developed, principally by John Whitney and Susan Howe, entitled *Religious Literature of the West* (1968). Initiated by the Pennsylvania legislature, extensively field tested, with national scholars of Judaism, Christianity, and Islam as consultants, it was to be followed by a similar elective course and textbook on Eastern religions. Notably during this period in 1969 there also appeared a wonderfully ambitious 1,000 page publication, *The Bible Reader: An Interfaith Interpretation*, which arose out of the "conviction that the preparation of citizens for life today requires an acquaintance with the Bible" (Abbott, 1969, p. ix). A review in *Time* stated:

> Indeed, perhaps the major problem many will find with *The Bible Reader* is its very abundance of thoughtful material. To cover the book thoroughly, or to expand on it, as the authors suggest, would probably take even the most heroic of teachers (and the most alert of classes) longer than a year of daily sessions. For most schools, the book could very well be spread out over two or three years – an option that the authors just may have intended (The Bible as Culture, p. 82).

Meanwhile, at Florida State University there began an ambitious effort to develop religion-study throughout the required social studies curriculum.

The Florida Project and its Challenges

In 1965 the State Department of Education in Florida created a State Committee on the Study of Religion in the Public Schools, which set out to explore creative possibilities for the relationship of religion and public education. The committee was in part Florida's answer to agitation by numbers of citizens at the Supreme Court decisions, which from they felt banished God from the public schools. Members of the diverse committee, parents, teachers, administrators, religious representatives, and educators, including yours truly as chairman, surprisingly agreed with the Supreme Court's decisions. Moreover, following the lead of the Honorable Justices, we decided that a curriculum development project focusing on the existing public school curriculum offered the most promise for enhancing religious literacy in public school education.

At Florida State we then began to develop a "religious issues" series for use as supplementary material in social studies courses at the high school level: ten units dealing with religious issues in American Culture, ten with issues in Western Civilization, and ten with World Cultures. After the materials were developed, they were tested in local schools by regular social studies teachers who participated in two six-week summer institutes with thirty social studies high school teachers in each. The materials, three volumes, plus teacher's manuals, were then published nationally by Addison Wesley (Spivey, Gaustad and Allen, 1972-76).

A second phase of the Florida effort was the development of four promotional films designed to introduce concerned citizens, school officials, and teachers to the educational possibilities for study about religion in public schools, including legal justification. These films depicted actual classroom instruction and showed engaged teachers and students learning about religion in non-partisan ways.

The third phase of the Florida project focused on the development of supplemental religion-study materials for use in the social studies curriculum at the elementary levels. This series, field tested nationally and published for use by schools and teachers, was designed to foster early appreciation and comprehension of religions. Even at the youngest ages, students can and should think about religion, understood broadly as story and way. At this level cross-cultural materials were used to help students become aware of how religion manifests itself in a variety of settings. Moreover, this early study about religion sought to accustom students to the inclusion of this subject as a natural part of classroom learning.

By the late 1970s, the Florida project, along with three other projects previously mentioned, had largely run its course, in part because of personnel changes and in part because of the less than enthusiastic response from schools, particularly administrators in high and low places. In addition, Florida's State Department of Education failed to support the efforts of its committee, especially the curriculum as developed by Florida State University's faculty. First, the State Department rejected an ambitious, detailed (perhaps overly so) state guide entitled, "Learning about Religion in the Florida Public Schools," which was prepared by our Florida State project and recommended unanimously by the state committee. Second, none of the curricular materials, developed by the FSU program and published nationally, were selected for the state-approved list of textbook and supplementary materials. That list was critical because state funds, the bulk of local school support, were then restricted to such approved texts.

In hindsight I am convinced that we could have been more politically adept. We failed to cultivate the right people. We also witnessed a failure of nerve: public school officials are too often, too easily anxious to avoid controversy. Further, we were ahead of our time, especially in that conservative religious folk were not then supportive of "objective" religion study in the public schools. It was school prayer or nothing. So it went.

Eight Commandments

In spite of disappointing results, I still maintain that we were basically on the right track. Consequently, I have distilled our experience (not for the first time here) into Eight Commandments for religion studies in the public schools. These are but one of many guides for such inclusion of religion-study.

(1) *Auspices of public school officials.* Study about religion in the public schools shall be under the auspices of public school administrators, teachers, local school boards, or state departments of education. Too often, efforts to introduce the study of religion in public schools are initiated and fostered by religious organizations or religious individuals. Consequently, there is justifiable fear by both nonreligious folk and religious minorities that the introduction of religion studies is a disguised attempt to indoctrinate or gain religious converts. Although criti-

cal advice of concerned groups – parents, teachers, representatives of major religious groups, students – is desirable, these folks should not be "in charge." Religion-study, like any and all other learning activities, is finally the responsibility of educational, not religious, leaders.

(2) *United States Supreme Court decisions.* Learning about religion shall build on the Supreme Court's decisions, which declared that religious *practices* sponsored by public school authorities are unconstitutional. Efforts to get prayer into the public schools are not a legitimate addendum of the program to further study about religion in the public schools. Precisely the people who want prayer in the public schools could be enthusiastic allies of religious studies – if they were to cease and desist from the *practice* issue. The *sin of omission* of the public schools is the absence of study about religion – not the absence of school prayer.

(3) *Curriculum development and teacher education.* The two key ingredients for learning about religion in public schools shall be exemplary curricular materials and competently educated and motivated teachers. It is unwise to expect that major efforts of curriculum development can be left to occasional attempts by well-meaning individuals. In the area of teacher education it is generally essential that teachers be regular public school teachers. The ready accessibility of clergymen or dedicated laymen should not be used as an excuse in the hiring of religion teachers. In regard to motivation, religion as a subject matter offers teachers stunning opportunities for getting students motivated, excited, and learning.

(4) *Religion and education.* Whenever religion studies are introduced or enhanced in the public schools, scholars from the area of religion and teachers from the social studies or humanities shall be collaborative, equal partners. Scholars in religion are needed because of general illiteracy about religion in the public schools and in the public at large. Educators are needed because religion scholars are primarily experienced at the level of higher education and have little knowledge of the school curriculum and of the developmental levels of students.

(5) *Existing curriculum and elective courses.* Religion study shall be incorporated <u>both</u> within already existing required

subject areas <u>and</u> in elective religion courses. On the one hand, the inclusion of religion materials within the regular public school curriculum, such as social studies or humanities, has distinct advantages. Such studies make use of regular teachers; moreover, regular students rather than a selective group of students are learning about religion. Further, by setting the study of religion into the existing curriculum, such teaching and learning are inevitably interdisciplinary. This emphasis protects against making religion into simply one more specialization engaged in the continuing battle to be added to an already overcrowded school curriculum.

On the other hand, most teachers are already set in their ways of handling social studies or the humanities. In addition, the supplementary approach faces the problem that most school textbooks virtually ignore the role of religion; therefore, the inclusion of religion necessitates additional costs – textbooks plus supplementary texts. Moreover, the introduction of religion-study by means of elective courses also has distinct advantages. Such elective courses give religion space, visibility, and a controlled way of getting people used to religion's being taught is a way that is proper to public school education. Further, the group of students who take such elective courses are there by choice, not compulsion; consequently, concerns of parents are minimized.

(6) *Use of primary sources.* Whenever possible, religion curriculum materials shall use primary sources, both verbal and nonverbal, including the media. Thereby, students are brought directly into contact with men and women who feel strongly about religion. They learn from those who are themselves involved, committed, earnest, courageous, penitent, caring, and persuasive as well as those who have used and abused religion as instruments of coercion, deception and contentment. This approach helps to avoid the danger of reducing the study of religion into a treatment of dates, names, places – simply the facts – and thus helps avoid the danger of making religion study dull and lifeless.

(7) *Inquiry approach.* Religion curriculum materials shall seek student involvement through stress on inquiry and discovery. Students should actively learn *from* religion rather than passively being taught *about* religion. The lecture method,

which often consists of passing on information, or at worst biased indoctrination, should be minimal. Instead, discussion, analysis, and role-playing should be maximized so that teacher and student learn together. This learning helps the student see that the phenomena under study have life and power. Thereby, students are led into wrestling with questions of transcendence, the sacred, moral principles, ethical considerations of conscience, freedom, responsibility, power, and justice – including not only the triumphs, but also the tragedies of religion.

(8) *Crosscultural approach.* Religion study shall be multicultural. Matthew Arnold is reputed to have said, "He who knows only the Bible, does not know the Bible." Knowledge about one's own religious tradition is insufficient to help students become liberated, educated. In order to become aware of the complexity, depth and breadth, highs and lows of one's own religion, the student needs to learn from the religious phenomena of others. Conversely, students should learn not only about other religions but also about their own. The argument that study about religion close at home is divisive builds upon the questionable premise that education in the public schools should aim exclusively at socialization.

The above eight commandments reflect the guidelines that we used for the development of curriculum materials and for teacher education in the Florida project. In a sense, these commandments defend the validity, if not the success, of our efforts; moreover, they provide workable practical guidelines for the future.

Because we focused upon social studies as the arena for our work, we were criticized for talking round and about religion and for failing to offer students opportunities for understanding the essence of religion. Admittedly, this criticism was more apt for the high school level issues series, which focused on ethical as well as religious issues. In the elementary level series we did a better job of getting very young students involved in understanding the essence and feel of religion.

The hope is that we are now entering a time in which citizens, scholars, and educators will unite in a common effort to reform public school education so that learning about and from religion becomes natural and pervasive.

The original Biblical Ten Commandments were of course followed by a period of wandering in the wilderness. Some day we in these United States are going to grow up and embrace the study of religion, including something like the imperatives of our Eight Commandments. Though such will not mean entry into the Promised Land, learning from religion in public schools will surely enrich the common life of our society.

Are we now at *some day*?

Before leaving the subject of religion-study in public schools, I want to put such efforts in a broader context, one that addresses why the current times are encouraging for religion-study in public education.

A first observation is that religion is currently prominent in public life, perhaps more so than at any time in our nation's history. In October of 2008 Douglas Hicks, director of the Bonner Center for Civic Engagement at the University of Richmond, wrote a memo to presidential candidates John McCain and Barack Obama calling for a religiously informed national leadership and a religiously informed United States citizenship:

> Devotion is a powerful force for good and for ill. Religious literacy, for lack of a better term, will be critical to your administration's success. Understanding the dynamics of spiritual and cultural identity – in the Middle East, Central Asia, India, and sub-Saharan Africa, for instance –- is correctly called the missing dimension in statecraft. And at home, the issues of homeland security, immigration, and economic health all require attention to religious and cultural differences.

> Thus one challenge of leadership will be to shape the public square in ways that encourage citizens to express their deepest commitments and still get along. So a big question when you become president will be, What messages will your leadership send to a *devout* and *diverse* citizenry? (2008, p. B14)

Once upon a time study of religion in the academy was characterized by three big empty, black holes: 1) the absence of religious studies departments in public universities, 2) the neglect of religion-study throughout the curriculum, and 3) the missing "Fourth R" of the study of religion in public (K-12) education. Thus far we have made significant progress only in the first area – departments of religion. In the second, religion across the curriculum, results are less than significant. And in the third, K-12, there are only tidbits to report. Why? What can we do?

In order to provoke rather than to prescribe I offer the following observations:

- The prominence of religion in public life offers an opportunity for religion-study in the public schools. No longer in the closet (the church or the family), religion, both its agony and ecstasy can and should be studied.
- Penn State University was on the right track – a course, "Religious Literature of the West," offers a great possibility for inclusion – not only because the "comparative" approach provides some much needed distance from the subject matter, but also because since 9/11 most citizens understand the urgency for learning about Islam.
- The limitations of the factual, historical critical approach for study about religion is increasingly recognized, even in Scripture study. Dale Martin's *Pedagogy of the Bible* (2009), though directed at seminary education, has implications for secular, public educational institutions.
- The strength and validity of the teacher of religion/scripture as facilitator is the principal subject of David Clines' 2009 presidential address to the Society of Biblical Literature (published 2010).
- Appreciative, creative, engaged learning from religion, including Scripture, should be the order of the day in K-16. As Peter Gomes (1996) advocates, learning from "the Good Book" must be "subtle, supple and modest" (p. 21).
- In our current – more than ever acknowledged – diversity there are no winners. Both the voices of the religious right and the secular left must be engaged and attended.
- The gorge that separates higher from K-12 education is ours to bridge. Contrary to popular belief, we have much to learn and everything to lose if we do not begin to collaborate (Weisbuch, 2008).

A retired Penn State American religion scholar emailed me the following comment:

> For what it's worth: I have felt for some time that we folks in religious studies have gone about attacking the task backwards. Don't you think the first step should be convincing appropriate units of universities (schools of education?) that our future public school teachers should be trained in religious studies? That superintendents and principals should be encouraged to hire those teachers? That professors in our field should make a greater effort to educate parents in what study of religion entails? Whatever the solution may be, we are paying a great price internationally for the widespread ignorance about religion from the highest counsels in the land to voters in the booth and cops in the street. (C. Cherry, personal correspondence, June 8, 2010)

In 2007, an international consensus emerged from a meeting held in Toledo, Spain. The resulting *Toledo Guiding Principles on Teaching about Religion and Beliefs in Public Schools* declared commitment to two core principles, "first, that there is positive value in teaching that emphasizes everyone's right to freedom of religion and belief, and second, that teaching about religions and beliefs can reduce harmful misunderstandings and stereotypes" (p. 12).

As stated earlier, religious literacy as a national goal needs to be addressed by three means: 1) college and university departments of religious studies, 2) interdisciplinary religion-study throughout the curriculum, and 3) religion study at all educational levels, kindergarten through graduate study. The deepest problem area is the one which affects the greatest number of students – K-12. There are many organizations that provide current resources and publications to support educators who strive to combat religious illiteracy. These include the American Academy of Religion, Bible Literacy Project, First Amendment Center, Office of Democratic Institutions and Human Rights, Pew Forum on Religion and Public Life, and the Society of Biblical Literature. (See the Appendix for a list of resources available from some of these and other organizations.)

Our story of model curricular and co-curricular projects that expand religion-study throughout the university represents a tiny blip on the higher education landscape. But if such grows and affects students in greater and greater numbers, then it can mean that more and more graduates and consequently more and more teachers in schools will be religiously literate and gifted, in turn, with the limitless task of educating citizens for discernment, tolerance, and understanding in the area of religion.

References

Abbott, W. M., S. J., Gilbert, A., Hunt, R. L., & Swain, J. C. (Eds.) (1969). *The Bible Reader: An interfaith interpretation.* New York, NY: Bruce.

The Bible as Culture. (1969, October 3). *Time*, 82.

Clines, D. J. A. (2010) Learning, teaching, and researching Biblical studies. *Journal of Biblical Literature.* Spring, 2010, *129*,(1), 5-29.

Gomes, P. (2002). *The Good Book: Reading the Bible with mind and heart.* New York: HarperOne.

Hicks, D. A. (2008, October 24). Memorandum to John McCain and Barack Obama. Subject: Leading a devout and diverse nation. The Chronicle Review. *Chronicle of Higher Education.* B14-15.

Martin, D. (2009). *Pedagogy of the Bible: An analysis and proposal.* Louisville, KY: Westminster John Knox.

Prothero, S. (2007). *Religious Literacy: What every American needs to know – and doesn't.* San Francisco, CA: Harper-Collins.

Spivey, R. A., Dye, J. G., Allen, R. F. (Eds.) (1976). *Learning About Religion/Social Studies.* Niles, IL: Argus Communications.

Spivey, R. A., Gaustad, E. S., Allen, R. F. (Eds.) (1972). *Religious Issues In American Culture.* Menlo Park, CA: Addison-Wesley.

Spivey, R. A., Gaustad, E. S., Allen, R. F. (Eds.) (1973). *Religious Issues In Western Civilization.* Menlo Park, CA. Addison-Wesley

Spivey, R. A., Gaustad, E. S., Allen, R. F. (Eds.) (1976). *Religious Issues In World Cultures.* Menlo Park, CA: Addison-Wesley

Spivey, R. A., Gaustad, E. S., Allen, R. F. (Eds.) (1972). *Teacher's Guide To Religious Issues In American Culture.* Menlo Park, CA: Addison-Wesley.

Spivey, R. A., Gaustad, E. S., Allen, R. F. (Eds.) (1973). *Teacher's Guide To Religious Issues In Western Civilization.* Menlo Park, CA: Addison-Wesley.

Spivey, R. A., Gaustad, E. S., Allen, R. F. (Eds.) (1976). *Teacher's Guide To Religious Issues In World Cultures.* Menlo Park, CA: Addison-Wesley.

Toledo Guiding Principles On Teaching About Religions And Beliefs In Public Schools (2007). Warsaw, Poland: OSCE Office for Democratic Institutions and Human Rights (ODIHR). Retrieved June 11, 2010, from the The Organization

for Security and Co-operation in Europe website: http://www.osce.org/
publications/odihr/2007/11/28314_993_en.pdf

Weisbuch, R. A. (2008, February 29). Creating a Third Culture. *Chronicle of
Higher Education.* Washington, D. C.: Chronicle of Higher Education. C2-
3,

Whitney, J. R., Howe, S. W. (1968). *Religious Literature Of The West.* Minneapo-
lis, MN: Augsburg.

Appendix

Resources on Religious Literacy and Public Schools

American Academy of Religion (www.aarweb.org/
PublicAffairs/ReligionintheSchools/default.asp):

Grelle, B and Naylor, K. (Eds.) (2002) Spotlight on teaching about religion in the schools. Atlanta, GA: American Academy of Religion. *Religious Studies News*. 17, 2, pp. 2-12.

Marshall, C. & Ambler, C. (Eds.) . Lesson Plans on Art, Religion and Popular Culture. Retrieved July 6, 2010 from the American Academy of Religion website: http://aarweb.org/Public_Affairs/Religion_in_the_Schools/Lesson_Plans/art.asp.

McAllister, S. & Moore, D. (Eds.) Lesson Plans on Religious Diversity and Pluralism in America Unit. Retrieved July 6, 2010 from the American Academy of Religion website: http://www.aarweb.org/Public_Affairs/Religion_in_the_Schools/Lesson_Plans/diversity.asp.

Program in Religion and Secondary Education (PRSE), Harvard Divinity School, offers graduate degrees in religion for secondary school licensure.

The Religion and Public Education Resource Center, California State University, Chico, offers professional development for public school classroom teachers.

First Amendment Center (www.firstamendmentcenter.org):

Haynes, C. (1999*). A Teacher's Guide to Religion in the Public Schools*. Nashville, TN: First Amendment Center

Haynes, C. & Thomas O. (2007*). Finding Common Ground: A first amendment center guide to religion and public schools*. Nashville, TN: First Amendment Center.

Leach, J. (Ed.) (2002). *A Teacher's Guide to Religion in American Life*. Nashville, TN: First Amendment Center

Lester, E. and Roberts, P. C. (2006). *Learning about World Religions in Public Schools: The impact on student attitudes and community acceptance in Modesto, California.* Nashville, TN: First Amendment Center

Teaching about Religion in Public Schools: Where do we go from here? (2003). Washington, D.C.: Pew Forum on Religion and Public Life and Nashville, TN: First Amendment Center.

The Bible and Public Schools: A first amendment guide. Nashville, TN: First Amendment Center.

Society of Biblical Literature (www.sbl.site.org/educational/ teachingbible.aspx): *Biblical Electives in Public Schools: A Guide.* (n.d.) Atlanta, GA: SBL Publications.

Levenson, D. (2003). University Religion Departments and Teaching about the Bible in Public High Schools: A report from Florida. *SBL Forum* (http://sbl-site.org.article ID=198).

Roncace, M. & Gray, P. (Eds.) (2005). *Teaching the Bible Through Popular Culture and the Arts.* Atlanta, GA: Society of Biblical Literature .

Roncace, M. & Gray, P. (Eds.) (2005). *Teaching the Bible: Practical strategies for classroom instruction.* Atlanta: GA.: Society of Biblical Literature.

Other:

Beal, T. (2009). *Biblical Literacy: The essential Bible stories.* New York: HarperOne.

Hubbard, J. (2008). *Schools Passing on Teaching Bible.* http://www.macon.com.

Johnson, L. T. (2006). A Bible Curriculum for Public Schools. *Christian Century,* February 21, 2006, pp. 31-37.

Kilman, C. (2007). One Nation, Many Gods. *Teaching Tolerance,* Fall 2007, 38 – 48.

Afterword – Lessons Learned, Looking Ahead

Miriam Rosalyn Diamond
Society for Values in Higher Education

The Religion and Public Life enterprise described in this book yielded rich and varied programs aimed at fostering student religious literacy. These initiatives demonstrated creativity and drew upon a variety of media and resources, from on-line videos and trips overseas to dialogues and service learning in the surrounding community and nature. The ventures illustrated that studying about faiths can occur in a variety of contexts – both in and out of the traditional classroom - and in conjunction with a range of disciplines. From political science to philosophy, health care to environmentalism, students had ample opportunity to explore the extensive role of religion.

The program creators identified learning outcomes they anticipated students would acquire as a result of participation. These goals reflected their school's mission and culture, as well as its setting. Some innovations, such as Florida State University's module on Islam and Berry College's courses on religion in American political history, emphasized the acquisition of knowledge leading to thoughtful and critical analysis of religion's impact on national and world events. Berry integrated the school's Christian identity into these outcomes, noting that:

Our goal was to help these students to have a more nuanced and sophisticated understanding of the Christian tradition and the various ways Christian thinkers have understood their faith as playing a role in political decision-making...We would like these students to think more carefully and respectfully about religious identity and how a democracy might respect discrete identities. We would like all our students to understand the complexity not only of their own tradition (or lack of tradition) but also of other religious faiths and traditions...

Another reason for introducing religious literacy programs was to promote skills that would enhance professional effectiveness. This was particularly evident in Bethel University's interfaith dialogue for social work students and the University of Missouri's Religious Literacy and the Professions course. Missouri's on-line course supported students in acquiring

...the knowledge necessary to behave appropriately in various religious settings; (the ability) to react and respond with greater sensitivity to cultural and religious issues they encounter among clients, patients, customers, co-workers, and their communities; (and skills) to engage more effectively in their personal and professional lives with those of diverse faiths.

A focus on the "Big Questions" regarding personal priorities and actions was at the core of Sewanee, the University of the South's Moral Development Living and Learning Community, where students considered

values held by various societies and cultures and ... their own process of decision-making and discernment, leading ultimately to informed engagement with the Sewanee and world communities.

At the same time, Colorado College's Environmental Stewardship course participants were asked to

Think of spirituality as that which grounds us by teaching us what this world is, and what our role in that world is. This course will explore spiritual understandings of the natural world and our human relationship with it and responsibilities toward it...How we can interact with and utilize the natural world and its resources sustainably will be examined.

University of the Pacific's "What is a good society?" Living Learning Community also demonstrated means of encouraging learners to explore their core principles and deeds. In addition, the interfaith sacred space and garden served to promote a sense of inclusion and connection among students.

Nurturing connections and communication on campus was also a goal of LaGuardia Community College's dialogues, alongside building relationships with the community in which the college is situated. Administrators found that

> Dialogues (at LaGuardia) are profound because they are not abstract flights of rhetoric, but grounded in the reality of face-to-face encounters across every imaginable boundary as students move between tradition and the quest to become New Americans...establishing strong relationships with a variety of faith-based community organizations and infusing material on religious diversity into credit and non-credit courses.

While LaGuardia is a public institution, students at faith-based Bethel University experienced similar means of cultivating ties with diverse neighbors in their metropolitan area. These discussions allowed students to build upon their religious education as they explored how their beliefs and values interplayed with the larger community.

The comprehensive Religious Studies program at Portland State sought to further student development along historic-political, philosophical, professional, and communal dimensions by helping students:

> ....investigate the relationship between religious beliefs and practices and the formation of culture, conceptions of human identity, and moral and ethical frameworks...investigate academically the diverse meanings of religious practices in human experience .... to broaden and deepen students' knowledge of religious traditions around the world, to foster an awareness of how religious discourses and practices affect the lives of individuals and societies, and to provide an opportunity for students to engage with diverse religious communities in the (surrounding) area.

Thus, a range of outcomes was established through these varied plans.

Faculty and administrators gleaned important insights in the process of designing the initiatives. Of significant note was the value of student involvement from the early planning stages. Learners provided a worthwhile perspective on how their peers view and engage with the issues at hand. Their feedback and suggestions increased the ventures' effectiveness.

Another message underscored was the necessity of attaining backing from constituents on and off campus in the process of introducing many of these programs. From alumni, advisory boards and foundations to institutional leaders and student activity groups, organizational support was key to many of these projects' success.

Because most of these courses, residences, and dialogues were pioneered during a national economic recession, innovators learned the importance of commitment and tenacity combined with flexibility in introducing change. The launching of several programs was delayed due to funding issues and resulting institutional restructuring. These educators' conviction that religious literacy is an essential ingredient of a complete education assured that projects remained on the agenda until they could be realized.

Where do we go from here? For one, it is necessary for students become critical consumers and providers of media coverage when in comes to issues related to religion. This includes traditional news sources, as well as the growing influence of technology as a medium of information and communication. For example, the University of Bridgeport offers a course on "Internet Religion" in which students "explore(s) how and whether the Internet as a medium is shaping the message of religion..." (Healey, 2010, p. 11). In order to do so effectively, students must have a basic understanding of the role of religion in general, as well as its "messages" as traditionally understood and conveyed. Such insight can have a constructive influence on the role students will take as both users and – as the internet becomes increasingly interactive - suppliers of knowledge.

Furthermore, as Robert Spivey argues, it is necessary to

educate the educators. Instructors at all levels should have ready access to credible resources on religion – both content and pedagogical approaches. It is important that teachers and faculty have opportunities to consider the intersection between faith and their own disciplines. These explorations may take place at campus workshops and in-services, conference breakout sessions, roundtable meetings, learning circles, reading groups, and specialized seminars similar to the Institute on Religion in Curriculum and Culture of Higher Education.

The Religion and Public Life programs described here represent a fraction of the number and range of those in place to address issues of religious literacy in educational institutions nationwide. This is a growing movement, despite some pockets of confusion and resistance. The initiatives detailed in this publication demonstrate that most common concerns can be met in a manner that preserves principles of academic integrity. We hope that religious literacy is on its way to inclusion in the American educational system across the board, resulting in a more aware and better informed society.

Reference

Healey, S. (2010). It Takes Discipline: Learning in a world without boundaries. *POD Network News*. Spring, 2010. 10 - 11.

Made in the USA
Lexington, KY
01 February 2015